The 77 Irrefutable Truths of Parenting

FOUNDATIONS FOR GODLY PARENTING

Larry Keefauver, D. Min.

YMCS
Your Ministry Consultation Services

© 2001 Dr. Larry Keefauver
Published by Your Ministry Counsultation Services (YMCS)
P.O. Box 950596, Lake Mary, FL 32795.
407-330-0410
407-324-5006 (fax)
lkeefauv@bellsouth.net

All quotes unless otherwise noted are from the New King James Version. Copyright„1979, 1980, 1982 by Thomas Nelson, Inc. Used by permission. All rights reserved.

An Equipping Publication of

YMCS

Your Ministry Consultation Services

ISBN: 1-893301-03-7 (pbk.)

Printed in USA.

Appreciation to:

Rev. Raymond Mooi and Li Meng,
and all the staff of The School of Acts & Acts Global Network

To Tom Gill,
my gracious and excellent editor

To my friend in Christ, Pastor Kong Hee,
who encouraged this ministry
and through whom Jesus shines brightly.

To my wife, Judi, who
taught me so much about parenting

To our wonderful children and children in love,
Amy, Lee, Peter, Tina, Patrick and Liz

To Mike and Marilyn Phillipps for their insightful
editing and Cathleen Kwas for design

To Dave and Janie Hail and all of the
Alliance Team for their support

And to our seed's seed,
Judah, Asher and Stone

Dedicated to the

Head of the Church—
Jesus Christ
Ephesians 1:22-23

List of Truths

Communication

1. Children require taking notice, talking, truth, trust, togetherness, touch, thanksgiving, time, teaching, Trinity.
2. Speak life not death to your children.
3. Only say what the Father tells you to say; only do what the Father tells you to do.
4. Talking *at* children is a monologue with the parent doing all the talking and listening.
5. Want a child to a to talk? Listen! Willing silence without interruptions primes a child's flow of communication.
6. Your child isn't a garbage can—no dumping!
7. Ask your child to share feelings not just opinions.

Discipline

8. Discipline corrects and teaches; punishment hurts and crushes.
9. Rules without relationship results in rebellion; relationship without rules results in chaos.
10. Consistency means parental warnings are always followed by immediate, appropriate correction.
11. Right behavior reflects right attitude.
12. Fearing a parent instills a spirit of deception and deceit; fearing God inspires respect for authority.
13. Contracts mutually agreed upon between parent and child prescribe consequences in advance.
14. Repentance must precede penance or change will never happen in your child's behavior or character.
15. Spare the rod; spoil the child. Appropriately applied pain to the butt gets a child's attention and associates wrong with pain instead of pleasure.
16. Because you "say so" doesn't make it so; because God "says so" makes it so.

17. Label behaviors not children.
18. Discipline allows short-term pain for long-term pleasure; permissiveness allows short-term pleasure for long-term pain.

Choices

19. Feelings arise, temperament may be inborn, but responses to feelings and thoughts develop attitudes and behaviors that are right or wrong.
20. Living to make children happy produces unhappy families.
21. Be proactive not reactive. Set rules and consequences in advance. The older the child the more the child participates in setting boundaries.
22. Solving problems for your children never teaches problem solving.
23. Answering your child's questions early deposits answers for their late questions when you're not around.
24. Counseling teenagers as a parent isn't advice giving; it's right questions followed by much listening.
25. When wrong, go to a child: admit it, quit it, forget it.
26. Teaching right from wrong considers the choice; compares to God; chooses the right; and counts the cost.
27. Teaching children purpose empowers them to plan.
28. Absolute truth is true for all times, for all places and for all people—parents and children included.

Example

29. You become an example when your word and way line up with God's word and way.
30. Parental authority is rooted in godly character not role or responsibility.
31. Instilling purpose in children prepares them for trials, tests and tribulation.
32. You're raising adults not kids.
33. Transparency will either make you a hypocrite or a hero depending on who a child sees behind your façade.

34. Without worship at home, your children will be unwilling to go out to a house of worship.
35. Integrity is what you do when you're unaware that you're children are looking and listening.
36. A parent is the first picture of God their children see.
37. Teach your children to discern between needs and wants by meeting their needs not their wants.
38. One of the greatest gifts a parent gives a child is character.
39. Quote God not clichés about Him to your children.
40. Get out of your child's way to God. Be a window to God not just a mirror of yourself.
41. Getting a child's respect requires giving respect.

Family
42. The goal of healthy families is interdependence not independence or dependence.
43. Healthy boundaries protect parents and children.
44. With increased responsibility comes increased privilege.
45. Divorce breaks both the hearts of God and children.
46. It's not about you...it's about your seed and your seed's seed.
47. Give your children to God and you'll always have them.
48. Purpose speaks to a child's potential; identity speaks to a child's destiny.
49. Promise-keeping builds trust on both sides of the fence.
50. In a child's mind: A car—$$$; A computer—$$; A designer item—$; You—Priceless!
51. Who children are *is* far more important than what they *do*. Children are human *beings* not human doings.

Love (Agape)
52. Unconditional love says, "There is nothing you can do that will make me stop loving you."
53. Right reactions arise from acting like God not just acting like our parents.

54. No substitute exists for quality, one-on-one time with children.
55. Your relationship with your child is often more important than your being right.
56. Replace criticism with affirmation.
57. Building on a child's strengths helps him/her overcome weaknesses.
58. Intimidation a child creates a fearful, angry adult.
59. Domination a child creates a weak, immature adult.
60. Manipulation a child creates a distrusting, controlling adult.
61. Forgiveness heals a child's hurts.
62. Speak to a child's heart not only about their behavior. Know your child's love languages.
63. Parenting for life is a given; friends for life is hard work.
64. The door of tough love must open both ways.
65. Forgive your child before he or she repents.

Blessing

66. Don't waste your tears; save them for a river of intercession and prayer.
67. A name of blessing is spoken daily over a child; a misnamed child lives with a daily curse.
68. Transgressing the Decalogue creates generational curses; obeying the Decalogue creates endless blessings.
69. The best way to teach prayer is to pray over, often and out loud with children.
70. Teach a child to manage money not credit.
71. Leave a spiritual and material inheritance great enough to bless your seed's seed.
72. Live to please God and bless ('esher) your children instead of blessing ('esher) God and pleasing your children.
73. Children need to learn that God not you is their source.
74. The fruit of the Spirit in a child grow from the seeds a parent sows.
75. Sow into your children to give them seed not only fruit.

76. The future of children is not determined by their past but rather God's plan.
77. Teach your child to choose blessing each day rather than curse.

The Reality of Parenting

"Train up a child in the way he should go,
and when he is old he will not depart from it." (Prov. 22:6)

An irrefutable truth is rooted in God's Word which
is true for all people, all the time, and in all situations.

A myth is true only some of the time,
for some people and in some situations.

Parenting myths abound.

Parenting rooted in God's truth is a precious legacy.
Parenting creates a sweet taste and a lasting hunger for God.

—Larry Keefauver

#1
Children require taking notice, talking, truth, trust, togetherness, touch, thanksgiving, time, teaching, Trinity.

It's impossible to parent part-time. Parenting requires our full-time attention, love, care, discipline, effort and excellence. Too often we try to squeeze parenting into a rushed, stressed schedule of work, recreation, personal development, entertainment and overlapping activities.

We confuse taking our children places and involving them in extra-curricula activities with involved parenting. Yes, part of parenting is going with them to their activities. But parenting is about relationship not just running around with children. What does a healthy, wholesome relationship with children look like? The foundation for training your children in the way they should go includes but is not limited the following:

The Top Ten "T's" of Training
1. **Taking notice**—Notice their clothes, hair style, non-verbal communication, friends, interests, change in habits, temperament, feelings, music, TV programs, video games, email, words, attitudes, behaviors, grades, hangouts, etc. In other words, notice everything.
2. **Talking**—Talk (which includes much listening) about feelings, thoughts, opinions, joys, hurts, random stuff, sexuality, finances, right from wrong, etc. Nothing is off limits. Talking with lots of listening communicates warmth, caring, interest, concern, love and empathy.
3. **Truth**—Tell your children the truth about God, morality, yourself, and the world around them.
4. **Trust**—Trust your children and be consistent so that they learn how to trust from trusting you.

5. **Togetherness**—Let you child know that you are "with" them not "against" them. You nor they are the enemy. As family you are working together not pulling apart.

6. **Touch**—Children need your physical touch—hugs, kisses, squeezes, and all kinds of appropriate touch.

7. **Thanksgiving**—An attitude of gratitude works both ways. Tell your children daily how thankful you are for them and they'll begin telling you the same.

8. **Time**—Children need you. Your presence cannot be replaced by stuff.

9. **Teaching**—Your are your child's primary teacher not the school, church, club, tutor, nanny or coach.

10. **Trinity**—A child's first picture of God is painted by a parent.

Train up a child in the way he should go, and
when he is old he will not depart from it. (Proverbs 22:6)

Action Steps I/We Need to Take

_____

_____

_____

_____

_____

_____

#2
Speak life not death into your children.

"I'm sorry. I really didn't mean to say that." Excuses after we have spoken death will not undo the damage of poison deposited into a child's heart.

Jesus reminds us that out of our hearts, our mouths speak. If we don't mean it, then we should not say it.

Think before you speak. Be certain that your words build up instead of tear down a child's life. Keep yourself accountable. For a week, write down a daily journal in which you log all the positive and negative statements you make to your child. Do the negatives outweigh the positive?

My rule of thumb is that is takes at least ten positive statements to remedy one negative remark. Do your critical remarks drain life out of you child and leave him or her empty, lonely, abandoned and hurting?

Speaking life into a child begins with acceptance and listening and overflows with affirmation, encouragement, edification, support and speaking significance into a child's daily walk. Instead of continual criticism, try positive correction and intentional compliments for a child's efforts to grow and mature.

Life speaks to a child's personhood, positive performance and potential. Death constantly points out a child's failure, mistakes and misguided thoughts, feelings and attitudes. You are not your child's accuser, judge or prosecuting attorney. You are your child's teacher, supporter, encourager and godly parent.

Death and life are in the power of the tongue,
And those who love it will eat its fruit. (Proverbs 18:21)

#3

Only say what the Father tells you to say; only do what the Father tells you to do.

"Where did that comment come from?" Ever wonder what the source of some of your remarks is?

I often found myself simply parroting to my child the stuff my parents repeated often to me. Some of it was positive but other comments really did more harm than good.

Jesus gave us a good model to follow. He only did and said what the Father told him to do and say.

In our parenting seminars with teenagers, we often have parents and youth give one another permission to ask, "Did the Father tell you to say that?" Or, "Did the Father tell you to do that?"

We need to begin listening more to God and less to our past voices, parent tapes or worldly quips. The more of His Word that we have in us, the more likely His Word is to come out of us.

When we listen first to God, we will be less likely to spout off some inane comment to our child that hurts and crushes the spirit. When we know what God wants us to do, we will avoid acting or reacting out of anger or emotional distress.

If we have a hard time hearing from God, we need to spend more time with God—in scripture, prayer, meditation, contemplation, worship, praise, silence and intercession. Wouldn't it be great if our children knew we had just been with God before we spoke into their lives? Wouldn't it be awesome if our children knew that our touch, our expressions, our words and our deeds were simply an extension of His?

Therefore, whatever I speak, just as the
Father has told Me, so I speak. (John 12:50)

#4
Talking at children is a monologue with the parent doing all the talking and listening.

"I'm tired of hearing myself talk." I can remember my mother frequently making this comment.

Frankly, she was talking but I wasn't listening. I had all of her "sermons" memorized. So when she turned on the message, I tuned out.

Failing to learn anything, I began preaching to my children. Then I discovered my children doing the same thing to me—tuning me out. Old habits are hard to break.

Parenting is not an endless succession of sermonettes or monologues that we play over and over again until they are indelibly etched on the minds of our children.

If you find yourself preaching more than teaching, talking more than listening, and using monologues more than dialogues, stop. Use questions and open-ended statements more than threats, dictums, dogmas and rules. And use "I" messages instead of "You" messages that tend to blame, project feelings and shut off meaningful dialogue.

Remember that the goal of a conversation with your child is to share not to "hit and run." We are often so busy and stressed that we deliver the monologue in a rush as we run out the door, drive out the driveway or quickly call on the phone. Our concern is to tell them what we want instead of to listen, share and really understand.

Put yourself to the test. The next time you are delivering a familiar monologue, stop mid-sentence and see if your child can finish the message. If she can, then you might say, "Will you forgive me for talking at you instead of talking with you?"

Don't ever forget that it is best to listen much, speak little, and not become angry. (James 1:19 TLB)

#5

Want a child to talk? Listen! Willing silence without interruptions primes a child's flow of communication.

"I can't stand it when he just sits there and looks at me." The teenager made this comment about the unbearable pressure he felt when his dad just sat silently in the room with him. No TV. No radio. Nothing else was happening except one-on-one relating.

How long will you wait to hear from your child? Are you willing to be silent until he speaks? Are you able to listen without interrupting what a child is saying even if their comments are painful to hear?

Three-year old Johnny was throwing a temper tantrum. I quietly said, "I will not listen to you if you act like this. When you get over your tantrum, come talk with me." Then I left the room responding to his negative behavior with silence. Later he meekly came to see me.

"I know you felt angry and frustrated. Now tell me about it without screaming and yelling," I coached. He talked. I listened.

Parental silence gives a child permission to speak without interruption. Teach a child to take responsibility for their feelings. It's not, "You make me feel...," but rather, "I feel...." Once a child has ventilated, then teach how to express feelings and thoughts in a respectful and kind manner. But you will never teach anything until you have first listened, understood and responded with edification instead of attacking what your child said.

Often my son and I would play golf together and go for long periods of silence. Just being together was enough. Then when he spoke, something really deep and significant would often surface. Silence can produce golden moments of communication.

A time to keep silence, and a time to speak. (Eccl. 3:7)

#6
Your child isn't a garbage can—no dumping!

Look into a mirror. Tug on your ear. Say out loud to yourself, "This is an ear not a garbage can."

The same is true for your child's ears. Refuse to dump your negative feelings about your spouse, your spiritual leader or your boss into your child's ears.

Never dump profanity into a child's ears.

Be careful not to let TV, radio, CD's, friends or computers fill your child's ears (or eyes) with garbage.

Guard the doorways into your child's life. Their eyes, ears, mouths and touch are sensory inputs that must be kept continually clean and pure by a parent.

We discovered that the phone was becoming a trash source for our children's ears. Monitor the phone. Set healthy boundaries to protect your children.

Some of the garbage we must keep out of our child's ears includes:
- Pornography
- Profanity
- Gossip
- Put downs
- Prejudice and racial slurs
- Hateful and angry remarks
- Backbiting
- Cursing

Just to name a few. I think you understand. The question is, *will you refuse to let your ears or your child's ears become garbage cans?*

Therefore, having these promises, beloved, let us cleanse ourselves from all filthiness of the flesh and spirit, perfecting holiness in the fear of God. (2 Cor. 7:1)

#7
Ask your child to share feelings not just opinions.

Too often I would ask, "What do you think?" Instead, I meant to ask, "What do you feel?"

Feelings speak to the heart while thoughts and opinions rattle around in the head.

Feelings get at our emotional responses, our raw gut-level reactions to people and situations. Feelings may arise out of temperament or conditioning. We can change our feeling responses but we must first get in touch with them.

Children first feel. Too often we teach them to cover up or hide their true feelings early in life. Then later, in the teen years, we wonder why they won't share their feelings with us.

Avoid saying, "Don't cry." Stop judging or critiquing the early feelings a child has. Teach a child to express feelings by taking ownership and responsibility for their feelings. Help a child identify the feeling. Are you feeling sad, angry, happy, excited, bored, etc.?

When children learn early how to share their feelings, they feel more comfortable later in childhood talking about how they feel not just what they think. Your child will learn how to talk about feelings from the way you share and handle your own feelings.

Feelings are an important part of who we are and how we relate to others. They are meant to be shared, examined, and openly expressed as long as we take responsibility for our own feelings. The next time you say to a child, "You make me so angry," apologize. Change your statement. "I feel so angry when...." Teach your child about feelings by responsibly sharing yours. Failure to share feelings can produce hard hearts in our children.

As he thinks in his heart, so is he. (Prov. 23:7)

#8
Discipline corrects and teaches; punishment hurts and crushes.

"I'm going to beat you until the sun goes down," the angry parent yelled at the abused child.

Punishment purposes to hurt because of hurt. When a child misbehaves, we discipline. Discipline corrects and teaches. Mr. Spoon is a resident at our home. He is a wooden spoon with a happy face on one side and a sad face on the other. As a neutral object, Mr. Spoon applies the rod of correction to the butt for the purpose of getting a child's attention and associating wrong with pain.

Never discipline a child when reacting emotionally in anger to his words or behavior. When a parent punishes out of an angry outburst, then the child only learns not to provoke a parent's anger.

Rebuke. Discipline uses rebuke first. A rebuking look or a word redirects wrong behavior or words into right responses. Rebuke allows a child to make correction before the embarrassment of wrong becomes exposed.

Chasten. Then comes chastening if rebuke doesn't work. Chastening makes public a private wrong. Chastening brings to light a wrong motive or attitude behind a child's words or behaviors. Chastening explains the wrong and teaches the right.

Scourge. This "strong" physical word when applied to the discipline of children doesn't imply hurting a child. Physical discipline like spanking, isolation, grounding, removal of privilege and enforcing previously set consequences becomes necessary when rebuke and chastening fail to turn a child to repentance. While controlled and limited spanking on the butt may work with young children, it fails to be effective after about six or seven. More reasoning accompanied by withdrawing privileges works best. Physical discipline applied simply to hurt a child or crush the spirit is abuse.

My son, do not despise the chastening of the Lord, Nor be discouraged when you are rebuked by him; For whom the Lord loves He chastens, And scourges every son whom He receives. (Heb. 12:4-5)

Action Steps I/We Need to Take

_____

_____

_____

_____

_____

_____

_____

_____

_____

_____

_____

#9
Rules without relationship results in rebellion; relationship without rules results in chaos.

Parenting is not about setting rules but rather building a relationship with your child. With a relationship, your child will never understand any rules or boundaries. Without understanding, a child looks for ways to rebel.

Your rules without you are meaningless. Your relationship with rules breeds confusion and chaos in a child's life. Rules establish boundaries that protect you and your children.

Your relationship with your child provides the bridge for communication, understanding, sharing and growing together. The key to your child's future success is a positive, healthy relationship with you that has boundaries for both of you.

A parent provokes a child to anger and rebellion when rules are arbitrary, inconsistent, without reference to God's truth, and enforced with power instead of love.

Rules foster rebellion when a child doesn't understand the reasons behind the rules or the consequences for breaking the rules. Excessive consequences to breaking rules teach a child that a parent can be unfair and unjust.

And now a word to you parents. Don't keep on scolding and nagging your children, making them angry and resentful. Rather, bring them up with the loving discipline the Lord himself approves, with suggestions and godly advice. (Eph. 6:4 TLB)

#10

Consistency means parental warnings are always followed by immediate, appropriate correction.

"Angie, I told you to stop touching that," mom warns.

"Angie, stop that right now, or else," mom threatens more loudly.

"Angie, if you don't stop, I will spank you," mom gravely announces even more loudly.

"Angie, right this minute stop or I will spank you. I mean it now," mom yells as Angie continues to ignore her mom.

How many times do you have to threaten before you child obeys? How loud much you get before your child pays attention to you?

Children learn when their parents' really *mean it*. Because parents fail to follow up their warnings with immediate correction, children learn to wait until the parent really means "business." You may be wasting valuable time and emotional energy with yelling and threatening.

- Give a calm warning stating the reason for it.
- Follow the warning with an announcement of the consequences if the child fails to obey.
- If the child continues to disobey, then take immediate action with implementing the consequences.

No yelling, screaming or stern threats are needed. The parent determines when a child will receive correction not the reverse.

Are you willing to take action after the first warning? Start this process when a child is young and as he matures, he will know that your warnings are serious the first time.

> *Discipline your son in his early years while there is hope.*
> *If you don't you will ruin his life.* (Prov. 19:18 TLB)

#11
Right behavior reflects right attitude.

How do you assess your child's attitudes? What they say doesn't always reflect what's in their hearts. You ultimately know a child's attitude by behavior not words.

Watch both their overt behaviors and their non-verbal communications. Note the following:

- Facial expressions
- Eye contact
- Body language—movement and position of hands and legs, gestures, etc.
- Tone of voice
- Touch or lack of touch

Describe behavior back to your child. When a child is acting inappropriately, let them watch their behavior in a mirror. Children need to learn to see themselves as others see them.

The goal of right behavior is servanthood. We live to serve God and others for His name's sake. Serving, obedient and giving behavior reflect a serving attitude. Talk is cheap. Actions speak far louder than words.

Jesus' parable of the two sons really summarizes this truth:

A man had two sons, and he came to the first and said, 'Son, go, work today in my vineyard.' "He answered and said, 'I will not,' but afterward he regretted it and went. Then he came to the second and said likewise. And he answered and said, 'I go, sir,' but he did not go. Which of the two did the will of his father?" They said to Him, "The first." (Matthew 21:28-31)

#12
Fearing a parent instills a spirit of deception and deceit; fearing God inspires respect for authority.

"I know my dad would kill me if he ever found out what I'm doing," confided the worried teenager.

Fearing a parent rarely instills obedience. In the early years, fear may serve to control a child's behavior. But as the child gets older, fear doesn't deter wrong behavior. Fear simply motivates an older child or teenager to hide their wrong behavior.

When a child fears a parent, a child does the right thing for the wrong reasons. Lacking a right attitude or obedient heart, a child soon learns to hide unacceptable and wrong behavior from the parent. A child's works hard not to get caught rather than to please God.

The motivation for making right decisions is a desire to obey and please God not simply to please a parent. Lacking the right motivation, a child who fears a parent simply avoids attracting the parent's attention. The child fearing "getting caught" learns to look good in front of a parent and the parent's friends so that the parents will not suspect wrongdoing.

Fearing parents instead of fearing God produces children that become deceitful and hypocritical. They play the "respect" game in front of their parents while doing whatever they like behind the parents' back.

Fearing God teaches a child to respect both God's character and his commands. Respecting, reverencing and desiring to please God motivate a child to be righteous. The child knows that God not only knows everything he does, but also knows every inner thought and motive.

Fearing God teaches a child that God wants the best for us and isn't trying to deprive us of what we need. Rather a child learns that fearing God produces the wisdom, knowledge and understanding to make the right decisions in a child's life. Right decisions produce in children the ability to prosper materially, relationally and spiritually.

A parent teaches *fearing* God by setting an example of holiness for a child. This example includes:

- Saying and doing only what the Father says and does.
- Loving and serving God heart, mind, soul and strength.
- Worshipping God with the child.
- Praying with the child.
- Never idly or vainly using God's name.
- Teaching a child God's Word.
- Living a morally pure life.
- Being consistent in discipline, keeping promises and obeying God's truth.

In other words, a child learns to fear God by watching us as parents. Judi and I have learned that children discover how to fear God by watching our lives.

The fear of the Lord is a fountain of life, to turn one away from the snares of death. (Prov. 14:27)

Action Steps I/We Need to Take

_____

_____

_____

_____

_____

#13

Contracts mutually agreed upon between parent and child prescribe consequences in advance.

"You're grounded for the next month," the irate parent screamed. Yes, the child had serious transgressed one of the rules. However, the parent has now created a bigger problem. Out of angry emotion, the parent has levied an excessive, punishing consequence. In reality, the grounding may only be for a few days, but the parent has appeared arbitrary and impulsive.

Contracts are proactive agreements made between parent and child. They state the expected behavior and also the consequence for violating the contract. Contracts may also state specific rewards for obedience. "When you come in on time, you have the privilege of _____. But when you come in late without getting permission, then you will suffer the consequence of _____."

A contract is simply an agreement reached between a parent and a child. Another word for contract is promise. The child promises to obey while the parent promises to hold the child accountable.

The contract clearly states the consequences for disobedience. This enables a parent to discipline and correct a child out of relationship rather than rashness.

Contracts allow a parent to put the responsibility on the child for both making right decisions and also for knowing the consequences in advance for disobedience.

Contracts allow parents to teach responsibility in advance. They also keep parents from overreacting in the heat of anger or disappointment. Contracting in advance avoids severe relationship conflicts if a problem arises.

> *My son, hear the instruction of your father,*
> *And do not forsake the law of your mother.* (Prov. 1:8)

#14

Repentance must precede penance or change will never happen in your child's behavior or character.

"I have to tell Angela the same thing over and over again," complained her mom.

A child simply doing the right thing isn't enough to effect lasting change. Only repentance brings true change in a child's life.

To repent means to change direction. Change is integral to repentance. Doing penance simply repeats an acceptable behavior. Penance is not guarantee of true change.

Billy said, "I may be sitting in the corner but I'm standing up inside." The outward behavior conformed to his father's expectation but his heart and mind wasn't changed. The very same behavior that sent him to the corner the first time will continually send him there. Why? Because nothing has changed inside of Billy.

Repentance not only means that Billy is sorry for his misbehavior, it also means that Billy has changed on the inside. Whatever was motivating his oppositional behavior has changed. He now is willing to comply with the set boundaries.

What brings repentance? Not one but many factors contribute to change in a child's behavior and character. First there is the confession of wrong and the acceptance of forgiveness. Then there is a decision not to do the wrong thing again. Finally, there's an ongoing inner desire within Billy to do the right and forget the wrong.

This whole process of change begins with an honest admission, "I am wrong." The admission isn't forced or coerced by the parent. It is a willing confession by the child that he is wrong and is willing to change both on the inside and the outside. Repentance leads to change and growth in a child's life.

Now I rejoice, not that you were made sorry, but that your sorrow led to repentance. For you were made sorry in a godly manner, that you might suffer loss from us in nothing. For godly sorrow produces repentance leading to salvation, not to be regretted; but the sorrow of the world produces death. (2 Cor. 7:9-10)

Action Steps I/We Need to Take

_____

_____

_____

_____

_____

_____

_____

_____

_____

_____

_____

#15

Spare the rod; spoil the child. Appropriately applied pain to the butt gets a child's attention and associates wrong with pain instead of pleasure.

Earlier I mentioned Mr. Spoon. When our children were young, we had a large wooden serving spoon and used it for our "rod of discipline." We travel extensively in southeast Asia. There the rod of correction is a cane. In other places, it is a neutral object meant to give minimal pain. The purpose of spanking a child on the butt is to:

- Get a child's attention.
- Help the child associate pain with wrong behavior.
- Interrupt a child's misbehavior.
- Precede a time of correction and teaching.

A spanking forces a young child to stop doing whatever wrong behavior they have been doing. A parent never spanks to hurt a child. Rather the spanking is a swat or two done to show a child that the parent is serious about stopping the wrong behavior, doing the right thing and receiving repentance from the child.

A spoon is a neutral object rather than a parent's hand. The butt is a soft, cushioned place that can receive a spanking without any physical damage. Long after a spanking has been forgotten, the child has learned to associate pain with wrong behavior. This is an essential life lesson to learn.

The end result is this attitude in an older child: "Wrong decisions and actions will hurt and damage my life." Spanking usually ceases around six or seven years of age when withdrawal of privilege becomes a much more effective means of discipline. Parents who spank out of rage and try to cause physical harm are abusive and should be reported to the authorities.

He who spares his rod hates his son, But he who loves
him disciplines him promptly. (Prov. 13:24)

#16
Because you "say so" doesn't make it so; because God "says so" makes it so.

Spock is not the ultimate authority on parenting. Nor is Dobson or any other person. The ultimate authority on parenting is God. *God is our Father.*

Our authority does not rest in our role or our position. God gives us an awesome responsibility for training up children. But that responsibility does not make us the final word on what a child should or shouldn't do.

"Daddy, why do I have to do that?" asked the child.

"Because I said so," responded the father.

No, our authority rests in the Lord who says what's right and wrong. Once we anchor ourselves in God, we have authority behind our answers. Without God, all we have is human opinion and reason.

For example, try saying this: "Child, the reason I insist that your room must be kept clean is because God is a God of order. He is always pure, clean and orderly." We must begin teaching about the character and nature of God early. True, child will not fully understand what we are saying. But the teaching will begin early and will stay consistent.

Not only do we expect our child to be orderly based on God's character, we also maintain our room and homes in an orderly and clean fashion. We are subject to the same authority as our children.

When our children see our lives line up with our teaching about God, then they will develop both a respect for and understanding of God and us.

The law of the LORD is perfect, converting the soul; The testimony of the LORD is sure, making wise the simple; The statutes of the LORD are right, rejoicing the heart; The commandment of the LORD is pure, enlightening the eyes; The fear of the LORD is clean, enduring forever; The judgments of the LORD are true and righteous altogether. (Ps. 19:6-9)

Action Steps I/We Need to Take

#17
Label behaviors not children.

"You're a bad boy," said the mother.

"Son, you're stupid," scolded the dad.

Labeling the child conveys the wrong message. We are building children up not tearing them down. We either speak blessings or curses over our children.

What we speak over children becomes self-fulfilling prophecy. Call children "bad" and they will become "bad." Label children "stupid" and they will become stupid. One gets what one speaks.

A physics teacher once told a class of just average students that they were the best students ever in that grade. All semester, the teacher reinforced that message. At the end of the term, everyone passed the course with flying colors. Why? They fulfilled the affirmation and blessing spoken over their lives.

"Child, you are a blessing, a gift from God, a wonderfully and fearfully made person whom God loves and wants the very best for," affirms the godly parent.

We need to label behaviors not children. We speak to a child's potential and destiny. We correct a child's attitudes and behavior. "What you have done is wrong," instructs the godly parent who then describes the wrong behavior and what can be done to correct it.

Call forth the God-given possibilities in your child. Let this be your child's affirmation learned from your lips:

For You formed my inward parts; You covered me in my mother's womb. I will praise You, for I am fearfully and wonderfully made; Marvelous are Your works, And that my soul knows very well. (Ps. 139:12-14)

#18
Discipline allows short-term pain for long-term pleasure; permissiveness allows short-term pleasure for long-term pain.

Immediate gratification is taught by our culture. We have fast foods, instant answers, and microwave meals. Our children learn from TV that major problems can be solved in half-hour sitcoms.

Gratifying our wants may bring momentary pleasure, but the fun it short-lived. Afterwards, the long-term pain can bring tragic consequences.

Instant credit brings long-term debt. Short-term sexual gratification can bring long-term sexually transmitted disease and emotional pain in a future marriage relationship. Short-term sugar brings long-term fat and the health problems associated with it. In other words, giving a child what she wants just to "shut her up" will never teach a child the virtues of patience, deliberate choice and long-term blessings.

Obeying a boundary and keeping a contract may delay a child's wants. But that obedience can meet a child's need for long-term maturity and spiritual growth.

However, discipline that teaches takes time, effort and patience. The fruit is character.

Permissiveness requires little thought, no patience and bring instant pleasure. However, the long-term fruit is lack of character in a child.

As a parent, be willing to pay the price of godly discipline. It may also cost you the short-term pain of time, hard work and consistent effort. However, the reward will be great. What you sow into the life of your child you will reap in a harvest of godly character.

And not only that, but we also glory in tribulations, knowing that tribulation produces perseverance; and perseverance, character; and character, hope. (Rom. 5:3-4)

#19

Feelings arise, temperament may be inborn, but responses to feelings and thoughts develop attitudes and behaviors that are right or wrong.

Dobson wrote about the "strong-willed" and the "compliant" child. That speaks of a child's temperament. Early in infancy temperament can be observed.

Some children quietly observe the stimuli around them. Others aggressively explore the same stimuli. Their temperaments emerge early in childhood. And the feelings that they express are often triggered by their temperaments.

An active, curious child frustrated in exploring his surroundings may become angry and cry. That's to be expected. But a child who continually becomes angry whenever frustrated develops attitudes and behavior that are wrong and need to be corrected.

William Carey, M.D., in *Understanding Your Child's Temperament*, identifies nine temperament traits that a parent can observe as either positive or negative: activity, regularity, initial reaction, adaptability, intensity, mood, persistence and attention span, distractibility and sensitivity.

As a child responds to your discipline, you will discover what's effective or ineffective in communicating right or wrong to a child. Simply saying "no" and explaining "why" works for some temperaments. Removing objects works for others while a spanking may be needed for some in order to learn what can be touched and what cannot be touched and "why" or "why not." Every child responds differently. We are like snowflakes not clones.

An emerging negative attitude or behavior needs correction early or a child will assume that the attitude or behavior is right. A parent is always observing, teaching, correcting and interacting with a child. Knowing and deciding what's right and wrong must be taught by a godly parent otherwise the child will learn from the world around them. That kind of experiential knowledge can lead to destructive consequences if a parent fails to teach and train a child in knowing right from wrong.

And these words which I command you today shall be in your heart. You shall teach them diligently to your children, and shall talk of them when you sit in your house, when you walk by the way, when you lie down, and when you rise up. (Deut. 6:6-7)

Action Steps I/We Need to Take

_____

_____

_____

_____

_____

_____

_____

_____

_____

_____

_____

#20

Living to make children happy produces unhappy families.

"Honey, does that make you happy?" asked the doting parent.

We live to please God not please our children. Children don't always know what's best for them. They rarely understand what they want versus what they need. They must be trained and taught by a godly parent.

Parents get their clue for parenting from God's word not from always trying to make their children happy. The truth is, parents can't make a child happy or sad. Children, like adults, are responsibility for their own feelings.

We can help children make right choices. We can teach children right from wrong. Children can learn that right choices made now can reap a harvest of long-term blessings and joy.

Too many parents try to bribe children with something that "makes them happy" for the moment. But the next bribe must always be bigger and better. The result will be long-term misery for both the child and the parent.

Please God, bless and teach your child. Happiness in life is not your goal or your child's. Knowing, serving and pleasing God is the goal.

Even so we speak, not as pleasing men,
but God who tests our hearts. (1 Thess. 2:4)

#21
**Be proactive not reactive. Set rules and conse-
quences in advance. The older the child the more the
child participates in setting boundaries.**

Too often, we find ourselves reacting to a child's negative
behavior and making "on the spot" decisions about what we say
and do. Our reactions often become overreactions which fail to
teach our child anything except that we're out of control of
ourselves.

Being proactive means...
• Contracts are set in advance
• Boundaries are drawn in advance
• Consequences are known in advance
• Reactions are appropriate to attitudes and behaviors
• Children have participated in both setting the rules
  and determining ahead of time the consequences

Being reactive means...
• Trying to make immediate decisions about correction
  and consequences
• Responding to our emotions instead of our child's
  needs
• Attempting to make quick decisions instead of implementing prior decisions
• Allowing our child to control and manipulate us
  under stress instead of letting God take control of an
  already anticipated possibility.

Have you ever discussed with your children what will happen
in correction and discipline if they...
• Lie?
• Fornicate?
• Become pregnant?
• Get arrested?

- Use drugs?
- Wreck the car?
- Steal?
- Skip school?

"We don't discuss such things because we don't want to be any ideas in their head," explained one parent.

The ideas and temptations are all around our child. We can proactively teach, set boundaries, establish contracts and equip our children to face their temptations, or we can react to disasters that arise out of ignorance, permissiveness, and lack of preparation. Choose to be proactive. Save yourself and your child a lot of grief!

For your family, be proactive like Joshua:

> *And if it seems evil to you to serve the LORD, choose for yourselves this day whom you will serve, whether the gods which your fathers served that were on the other side of the River, or the gods of the Amorites, in whose land you dwell. But as for me and my house, we will serve the LORD.* (Joshua 24:15)

Action Steps I/We Need to Take

_____

_____

_____

_____

_____

_____

#22
Solving problems for your children
never teaches problem solving.

"Don't do that," repeated the mother hundreds of times a day.

She was frustrated. The child became resistive and oppositional to everything the mother said.

The whole cycle of unproductive, ineffective parenting could
be reversed with a question instead of a demand. "Why are you
doing that?"

Early in childhood, a parent needs to teach a child to make
simple right from wrong decisions. A child has to think for
himself. But problem-solving skills are not caught, they are
taught.

First, they're taught by example. A child observes a parent
making right decision and learns by imitating the parent.

Then, problem-solving skills are taught verbally. A parent
goes through their process at arriving at a solution and answers a
child's questions about the process all along the way.

Finally, a parent plays back for a child what a child did in
solving a problem. The positive and negative steps in solving a
problem are explained, examined, and if need be, corrected.

Admittedly, teaching a child to solve a problem initially takes
a lot of time. But time and grief is saved in the long-term because
a child will learn how to do make right decisions for themselves.
We're not training up our children to cope. Coping means surviv-
ing in spite of the problems. Coping allows the problems to go
unsolved falsely believing that in time they will simply go away.

Solving problems means that children learn to take steps now
that will ultimately lead out of the problem and into a solution.
Solutions don't happen instantly. But step by step, any problem
can be solved with God's help, parental guidance and a child's
willingness to learn. The time worn but true cliché says, "Mile by
mile, life's a trial. Inch by inch it's a cinch."

I know how to be abased, and I know how to abound.
Everywhere and in all things I have learned both to be full and
to be hungry, both to abound and to suffer need. I can do all
things through Christ who strengthens me. (Phil. 4:12-13)

Action Steps I/We Need to Take

_____

_____

_____

_____

_____

_____

_____

_____

_____

_____

_____

_____

#23
Answering your child's questions early deposits answers for their late questions when you're not around.

Answering "why" early saves sorrow later.

"Johnny's questions seem endless."

The early years of childhood are filled with a curious stream of questions about why. Once you have repeated the same answers over and over again, repeat the questions and see if your children have "gotten it."

Deposit truth early in your child. Later in life when you're not around, your child will have a reservoir of answers to their ongoing questions about self, life and God.

Without your early truthful answers, a child will mature without foundations and virtue. The world offers too many wrong answers to life's important questions. Children are bombarded with TV, video, music, computer, school and peer answers to life's questions. But drinking from those often contaminated and polluted wells can produce stinking thinking and bad attitudes.

Your truthful answers, rooted in God's Word, given early in a child's life produce deep wells of living water from which a child can drink for a lifetime.

Young people can live a clean life by obeying your word. I worship you with all my heart. Don't let me walk away from your commands. I treasure your word above all else; it keeps me from sinning against you. (Psalm 119:9-11 CEV)

#24

Counseling teenagers as a parent isn't advice giving; it's right questions followed by much listening.

"Dad is always preaching at me," complained the son.

Sermonettes rarely communicate lasting truths. Children are much more inclined to listen after they have been listened to. Are you willing to ask the right questions and then listen to your child's answers? And remember that a child's initial response, decision or problem may not be the real feeling, thought, attitude or problem.

Take time to ask these questions two or three times. Listen to your child's response. Don't interrupt. Paraphrase back what your child is saying. Reflect back his feelings to be certain you understand. After listening, then give godly wisdom filled with positive responses, options and possibilities. An impossibility thinker has few options, none of which will work. A possibility thinker has a long list of wise choices, some of which will work.

Ask your child:

> *What do you want for you?*
> *What are you feeling?*
> *What are you doing about it?*

After going through these questions a few times asking your child for a different set of answers each time, then ask, "What will you do?" Help your child explore positive possibilities with these questions:

> *What does God want for you?*
> *What is God feeling about you?*
> *What does God want you to do?*

Make a first step. Ask, *Will you do what God wants? When will you? How will you? Why will you do what God wants?*

Get ready. This will take time but the seed that you sow in listening and counseling a child will bear a harvest of righteousness, joy and peace.

Now may the God of hope fill you with all joy and peace in believing, that you may abound in hope by the power of the Holy Spirit. (Rom. 15:13)

Action Steps I/We Need to Take

_____

_____

_____

_____

_____

_____

_____

_____

_____

_____

#25
When wrong, go to a child: admit it, quit it, forget it.

The hardest three words a parent may ever have to say to a child are, "I was wrong."

However, such confessions can build trust and intimacy between parents and children. We train our children to confess their wrongs by modeling such confession ourselves.

At times, we will react emotionally and rashly to our children's behaviors and attitudes. In the stress of the moment, we may do or say things that we know are wrong. Such situations call for quick and immediate repentance. Children learn how to repent by imitating our repentance.

Admit it. When wrong, say, "I was wrong when _____. Will you forgive me?" Teach your child to say the same thing.

Quit it. Stop doing what's wrong. Change your wrong behavior and attitude. The fruit of sincere repentance is a change in direction. We stop doing what's wrong and begin doing what's right. Teach your child that true repentance means that he stops doing what's wrong.

Forget it. Neither you nor your child has permission to bring up past sin that have been confessed and forgiven. A past failure doesn't make a person a failure. Let go of the past. Don't bring it up to accuse or condemn yourself or your child. Teach your child to forget and let go of their past failures and mistakes as well as yours.

Remember that forgiveness is not an option. Jesus commands us to forgive (Matthew 6). Asking for a child's forgiveness helps them to keep unforgiveness out of their lives.

Confess your trespasses to one another, and pray for one another, that you may be healed. (James 5:16)

#26
Teaching right from wrong considers the choice; compares to God; chooses the right; and counts the cost.

"Dad, why do you have a radar detector in your car?" queried the teenage son.

We insist that our children obey God's laws and the laws of the state. We demand that they respect God-ordained authority. But do we teach them what's right by both example and lifestyle?

If it's all right for me to break the speeding laws, then it must be alright for my son to follow my example. Making right decisions is rooted in absolute truth as revealed in the God of truth. His character is truth. Our character as parents must reflect God's nature.

The steps in teaching children to make right from wrong decisions are detailed in the adult curriculum (Lifeway) I wrote for Josh McDowell's book, *Right from Wrong*. Here's a summary:

1. **Consider the choice.** Step back from the decision and consider all the choices facing you.
2. **Compare to God.** Determine which choice(s) line up with God's nature and truth.
3. **Choose the right.** When you know what is right, do it.
4. **Count the cost.** Understand that right choices may result in short-term pain and long-term gain. Wrong choices often bring immediate please and self-gratification but result in a long-term harvest of sorrow and pain.

As a parent, you cannot anticipate every decision your child will have to make. In our complex world, children are faced with important decisions daily. They must decide whether or not to obey their parents. Then they must decide about what to listen to, watch, read or play. The choices are almost endless. Equip your child to make right choices based on the character of God.

*For before the Child shall know to refuse
the evil and choose the good.* (Isa. 7:16)

Action Steps I/We Need to Take

_____

_____

_____

_____

_____

_____

_____

_____

_____

_____

_____

_____

_____

#27

Teaching children purpose empowers them to plan.

"What's your purpose in doing that?" asked the parent.

Help your child write a purpose statement for their life. As they grow older, the purpose statement may expand. Jesus indicates that primary purpose is loving God wholeheartedly and loving others and ourselves fervently. Are you willing to teach that to your children?

A simple purpose statement may be:

I am loving God by _____.

I am loving others by _____.

I am loving myself by _____.

Any plan that lines up with my purpose is *on purpose*.

Any plan that contradicts my purpose if *off purpose*.

"So Johnny, how does taking Billy's toy show Billy that you love God and him?" asked the godly parent. Johnny has been learning from his parents that loving God and others comes before loving self. Johnny must now plan to return Billy's toy and apologize.

As a teenager, Johnny begins to make life decisions based on his purpose. Those plans reflect God's will because they are on purpose. Scripture declares that there is a "time for every purpose under heaven" (Eccl. 3:1). Help your child discover purpose before they make plans about the future.

Jesus said to him, " 'You shall love the LORD your God with all your heart, with all your soul, and with all your mind.' This is the first and great commandment. And the second is like it: 'You shall love your neighbor as yourself.' (Matt. 22:37-40)

#28
Absolute truth is true for all times, for all places and for all people—parents and children included.

"If it's true for you, it's true for me," instructed the parent.

We cannot teach what we do not life. We cannot say, "Do as I say, don't do as I do."

God wants us to be consistent as well as truthful. Why? Because true is consistent. The world teaches children relativism. But Scripture teaches absolute truth.

Absolute truth is universal—it's true for all people and in all places.

Absolute truth is constant—it's true for all times.

To model truth, a parent has to be consistent about truth every day. The boundaries haven't changed just because it's a new day. The reality of right and wrong is just a true for parents and for children. Parents cannot lie. Nor can children.

Are you will to live a life of absolute truth?

And you shall know the truth, and the truth shall make you free. (John 8:32)

Action Steps I/We Need to Take

_____

_____

_____

_____

_____

#29
You become an example when your word and way line up with God's word and way.

"Are you Jesus?" the child asked me.

I was teaching a Sunday school class when a four year old asked me this revealing question. Authority figures are all in the same concrete, mental category for a child. All are good or all are bad. Since I was in authority, then I must be good just like Jesus.

It's difficult for a child to imagine the invisible or to distinguish between fantasy and reality. Children are concrete thinkers. So, I must represent all that Jesus is or does. A parent is the first picture of God a child sees.

The character transfers from my personality to God's are almost automatic for the young child. If I yell, God must yell. If I am critical, God must be critical. If I love, God must love.

As a child matures, he begins to distinguish between God and a parent. If a parent's actions conform to God's character, then a child isn't confused when a parent teaches and trains him in right or wrong. But if glaring inconsistencies exist or if the parent never admits to being wrong, then a child faces a moral dilemma. *Who am I to trust? God? My parent? Neither?*

Paul writes, "Imitate me as I imitate Christ" (1 Cor. 11:1). That's bold. That's real. That's the way parents must life out life before their children.

Be an example to the believers in word, in conduct,
in love, in spirit, in faith, in purity. (1 Tim. 4:12)

#30

Parental authority is rooted in godly character not role or responsibility.

"As long as you live under my roof, you will do I what tell you to do. I brought you into this world and I can take you out of this world," the irate mother yelled.

Authority is vested in relationship not role. I exercise authority as a parent because God set me in place as a parent and gave me the responsibility and authority to minister to my children on His behalf.

Children are a gift not a possession. As parents we are stewards of the awesome gift from God called a child. We are held accountable for how we invest our gifts in the kingdom of God.

Like Abram, *we are blessed to be a blessing.* As such, we pour the seeds of material, emotional and spiritual blessings into our children expecting the fruit of God's spirit to be produced in their lives. Our personal, dynamic relationship with the Lord empowers us to exercise His authority as well as His justice and mercy in our child's life.

We are physical giants in the eyes of a child. At first, they see us as threatening, overwhelming, huge creatures who can overpower them in every way. Exercising authority arbitrary and in a heavy handed way intimidates a small child. But we can be loving, gentile, fair teachers of truth who communicate God's ways to a child. As such, God's authority and character will shine through us.

Parental authority is imparted by the Spirit of God not inherited from our parents. Parental authority is exercised on God's behalf. We exercise his authority, his way, in his time, for his purpose so that God can be see in and through us.

You know that those who are considered rulers over the Gentiles lord it over them, and their great ones exercise authority over them. Yet it shall not be so among you; but whoever desires to become great among you shall be your servant. And whoever of you desires to be first shall be slave of all. For even the Son of Man did not come to be served, but to serve, and to give His life a ransom for many. (Mark 10:42-45)

Action Steps I/We Need to Take

_____

_____

_____

_____

_____

_____

_____

_____

_____

#31

Instilling purpose in children prepares them for trials, tests and tribulation.

Are you problem focused or purpose focused?

Problem-focused parents always concentrate on the child's problems. They constantly worry about the child's attitudes and behaviors. They suffer great anxiety over a child's performance in sports and in school. Anything a child does or says that falls the least bit short of their expectations becomes a crisis for the problem-focused parent.

On the other hand, the purposed-focused parent knows that trials, tests and tribulations are just passages to the next level of prosperity and success in a child's life. The light afflictions of life simply work a greater glory in our lives and our children.

Mountains that we climb together are not the problems only the means for strengthening us for the next climb. Jesus reminds us that only a tiny amount of faith—which means *trust*—is needed to move mountains. A bond of trust is built between a parent and a child who know God's purpose for their lives.

Purpose sees through the trials to the victory. Purpose understands that tests are simply opportunities to pass through to a higher level. And tribulations are merely workouts that strengthen us for the weight of glory that we will bear. When a child sees a victorious, overcoming, ever-growing, stronger parent pushing through with them on purpose, that child will grow in their own purpose to a place where their on-purpose, God-given plans will push them through from one breakthrough in life to the next.

Therefore we do not lose heart. Even though our outward man is perishing, yet the inward man is being renewed day by day. For our light affliction, which is but for a moment, is working for us a far more exceeding and eternal weight of glory, while we do not look at the things which are seen, but at the things which are not seen. For the things which are seen are temporary, but the things which are not seen are eternal. (2 Cor. 4:16-18)

#32
You're raising adults not kids.

"When I get my kids raised, I will take life easy," the misguided parent shared with me.

Raising kids produces immature people is grown-up bodies. I have met 50-year old kids running around still treating others and God in childish ways.

God is calling you, as a parent, to raise adults. By the time children reach the teen years, you should have young adults living with you who can...

- Handle money and a budget responsibility. They could manage your household bills and budget if you needed them to do so.
- Work as a volunteer or for pay with integrity and productivity.
- Take responsibility for their feelings, thoughts and behaviors.
- Keep promises, fulfill contracts, and discipline themselves.
- Be your friend, confidant, and colleague in ministry.
- Serve others humbly and effectively.
- Pray, minister, share, study the scriptures and witness to their faith.
- Be trusted to choose friends who edify and encourage them.
- Make right decisions consistently.

Teenagers can be responsible friends to their parents holding one another to mutual, righteous accountability. But this only happens when a parent proactively plans to train a child in the ways of God instead of produce another consumer in today's materialistic culture.

Make the decision now. When your child is twenty, do you want a child in an adult's body?

When I was a child, I spoke as a child, I understood as a child, I thought as a child; but when I became a man, I put away childish things. (1 Cor. 13:11-12)

Action Steps I/We Need to Take

_____

_____

_____

_____

_____

_____

_____

_____

_____

_____

_____

_____

_____

#33

Transparency will either make you a hypocrite or a hero depending on who a child sees behind your façade.

"My parents really act differently at church than at home," confided the teenager.

After twenty years of counseling families, youth ministry and talking with teenagers, I learned much about facades. The face that parents and children put on at church can be quite different from what goes on at home behind closed doors.

Parents or children might be able to fool a pastor some of the time, but they know the truth about one another. Judi and I had a rocky season in our marriage. At times we had verbal disagreements which our children overheard. One day our youngest son came home and asked at dinner, "Dad, are you and mom going to get a divorce?"

We were shocked at his questioned. We had briefly considered a divorce but never mentioned it to the children. Patrick confided, "Most of my classmates have parents who are divorced. They said it started with verbal fights like you and mom have sometime. So, I thought you might be getting a divorce too."

Children really know what's going on in a marriage or a family. We cannot hide behind facades with our children. At times their intuition tells them about family problems even when those problems aren't verbalized by the parents. What kind of person do your children really see at home?

Do you children see the Lord shining through you? Are you a reflection of His glory? Or is the window of your life so dirty that Christ in you is distorted?

But we all, with unveiled face, beholding as in a mirror the glory of the Lord, are being transformed into the same image from glory to glory, just as by the Spirit of the Lord. (2 Cor. 3:18)

#34
Without church at home, your children will be unwilling to go out to church.

"My kids hate going to church," confessed a mother. "I just don't know what to do with them."

That's always my first clue that the spiritual climate of a home is terrible. Church is not a place; it's a community. Being the family of God starts at home. If children do not experience God's presence at home, they will find worshipping with the larger family of God very difficult.

Paul writes in 1 Corinthians 3 and 6 that we are the temple of the Holy Spirit. That being the case, worship must happen at home. We are a royal priesthood. As such, we are to minister to the Lord all of the time. But are we?

Parents set the spiritual atmosphere and control the spiritual climate of the home. Their passion for Christ or lack of it sets the thermostat for worship in the home.

How can you have church at home? Consider these possibilities:

- Play spiritual music at home continually.
- Talk about the Lord often in your conversation.
- Give God praise continually even in the little things.
- Pray daily blessing over your children.
- Have a family devotional and sharing time. Let children take leadership in this. Share don't preach.
- Let the joy of the Lord fill your face and your voice.
- Play scripture tapes.
- When the TV is on, tune it to Christian music videos or teaching.
- Pray about problems together.
- Pray with your children in the morning, at meals and in the evenings.
- Play Bible games together.

- At church, worship together and find intergenerational settings in which to learn together.

And these words which I command you today shall be in your heart. You shall teach them diligently to your children, and shall talk of them when you sit in your house, when you walk by the way, when you lie down, and when you rise up. You shall bind them as a sign on your hand, and they shall be as frontlets between your eyes. You shall write them on the doorposts of your house and on your gates. (Deut. 6:6-9)

Action Steps I/We Need to Take

_____

_____

_____

_____

_____

_____

_____

_____

_____

_____

#35

Integrity is what you do when you're unaware that you're children are looking and listening.

"I could just kill that dog," exclaimed our grandson as the bothersome dog across the street from his home kept barking.

Our daughter was shocked by her three-year old's statement. Where could he have gotten such a violent idea? Then she remembered muttering just the same words only a few days before when the howling dog had jarred her youngest son prematurely awake from his afternoon nap. She hadn't realized that her older son had been in the next room and overhearing her strong invective.

Your child is observing your every move and listening to your every word at home. You may forget that your child is around. But a child's life silently records a parent's life. Then at the most unexpected time, a child will speak or act *just like us.*

We may guard our hearts, our tongues and our actions when we consciously know our child is looking. But what about those times when we go through our customary routines without thinking about how we sound or look to our child?

Integrity is who we really are on the inside. Integrity is what we do when we think no one is looking. The person our child becomes like is not the outer person but the inner person we are. The real you is who your child will become. Is the real you more like God or more like the world around you?

Are you willing for a child to repeat anything you say in private?

Are you willing for a child to model any of your behaviors?

But as for me, I will walk in my integrity;
Redeem me and be merciful to me. (Ps. 26:11)

#36
A parent is the first picture of God their children see.

This is a good place for a self-test. What kind of picture is your child seeing? John writes that *God is love*. So the portrait of God a child sees in and through you must be anchored in love.

So let's go to 1 Corinthians 13. This chapter defines the unconditional love of the father that fills and flows through our lives into our children. Put an "x" on the line that reflects where you are right now in communicating love to your children.

Love is patient, love is kind. It does not envy, it does not boast, it is not proud. It is not rude, it is not self-seeking, it is not easily angered, it keeps no record of wrongs. Love does not delight in evil but rejoices with the truth. It always protects, always trusts, always hopes, always perseveres. Love never fails. (1 Cor. 13:4-8 NIV)

My attitude and actions toward my children are:

Patient	Impatient
Kind	Mean
Humble	Arrogant
Mild-tempered	Angry
Forgiving	Unforgiving
Protecting	Exposing
Constant and reliable	Inconsistent
Unconditional	Conditional

Are your children seeing God through you or are you blocking the view? Loving children with the love of God means that you seek the best for your children. It's your desire that their deepest needs are met.

And in loving your children, you model for them how to love others unselfishly. Do your children experience the Father's love through you?

> *And now abide faith, hope, love, these three;*
> *but the greatest of these is love.* (1 Cor. 13:13)

Action Steps I/We Need to Take

_____

_____

_____

_____

_____

_____

_____

_____

_____

#37

Teach your children to discern between needs and wants by meeting their needs not their wants.

"Mommy, can I get this?" the young child pleads holding a toy pulled off the store's shelf.

"No, you can't have it. Put it down," scolds the mother.

Immediately a big struggle erupts in the middle of the store, as the child throws a temper tantrum. His behavior dares the mother to discipline him in public. Trying to quiet the child, the mother gives in to the child's wants.

This typical scene gets replayed millions of times each day between parents and children. When a parent sets boundaries for a young child, the parent needs to be proactive. That means that the parent and child understand what lies within the child's boundaries of needs. Children can learn to express needs like:

"I'm hungry. When can we eat?"

- "I'm thirsty, may I have a drink?"
- "I'm cold. I need a coat."
- "I'm tired. I need to rest."
- "I'm bored. I need to be involved."

Parents can respond to such needs by meeting them or explaining what will be done to meet the need. Within a child's boundaries are acceptable actions and attitudes that bring blessings. The parent doesn't fill a child's boundaries with don'ts. Rather, the majority of teaching and training needs to focus on dos. For example, *you need to rest when you are tired. You need to eat food that's good for your body. You need to get involved in a fun, creative activity when you are bored.*

Avoid focusing on instructions like: *Don't get out of bed. Don't eat candy. Don't move when I tell you to sit still.* Look for ways to meet a child's needs instead of gratifying his wants just to keep him "out of your hair."

A life filled with don'ts for a child becomes very frustrating. Focus on what a child can do and have in meeting their needs instead of what they can't do and have to get what they want. Wants are based on immediate urges that aren't necessary for a child's physical health and safety or his emotional or spiritual well being.

Like our heavenly Father, we meet the real needs not the momentary whims or wants of a child.

And my God shall supply all your need according to
His riches in glory by Christ Jesus. (Phil. 4:19)

Action Steps I/We Need to Take

_____

_____

_____

_____

_____

_____

_____

_____

#38
One of the greatest gifts a parent gives a child is character.

"You act just like your dad," my father's friend said to me.

I'm not sure to this day if that was a good thing or not. Some of my father's traits were commendable but other's like chewing tobacco weren't so great.

The most transparent father in the Bible is probably Joseph, Jesus' earthly dad. Joseph was so transparent, that Jesus saw the Father clearly through his dad. Jesus was always acting like his heavenly father.

We can infer that Jesus must have spent a lot of time with Joseph in the carpentry craft growing up. We know that a young boy in Jesus' day would have learned the Torah sitting at the feet of his father. He must have learned it well for Jesus continually quoted the scriptures. However, I can't think of a time that Jesus ever said, "My daddy said...."

Here's the point: As *parents we want to impart the Father's character to our children not our carnal natures.*

In fact, there are times when we must say to our children, "That was me speaking. That wasn't the Father speaking to you."

I'm pure because the Father is pure. And I desire to teach purity to my children so their character is morally pure. Let it be your desire to imitate Christ, to be like the Father, to walk in the Spirit as much as possible. And when you don't, give your child permission to ask you, "Where did that statement or action come from—the Father or you?"

Character filled with the virtue of God and the fruit of the Spirit is the most precious gift we can give our child. When we give our child Jesus, we imitate Christ in such a way that they see more and more of Him and less and less of us.

He must increase, but I must decrease. (John 3:30)

#39
Quote God not clichés about Him to your children.

Can you recall all the Scriptures that your parent taught you as you were growing up? In only a few instances have I met adults whose lives are filled with God's word based on the Word spoken into and over their lives by parents. On the other hand, I rarely meet an adult who can't quote a least a dozen clichés that parents frequently showered on them as children.

For example, can you complete some of these that my parents often quoted to me?

Cleanliness is next to _____.
If a thing is worth doing, it's worth doing _____.
Don't start something you're not willing to _____.
I brought you into this world and I can _____.
You're driving me _____.
As long as you live under my roof _____.
Children are meant to be seen and not _____.
God helps those who _____.
A penny saved is a _____.

You probably could complete most of these archaic parent tapes. But if I quoted for you some of the most important "John 3:16" type memory verses, could you complete them?

My point here is simple. Focus on teaching, speaking and quoting God's Word instead of trite words of men.

Your word is a lamp to my feet
And a light to my path. (Ps. 119:105)

#40

Get out of your child's way to God. Be a window to God not just a mirror of yourself.

"I'll never follow Christ. My pastor father abused me and I refuse to set foot inside of a church," confided the wounded daughter of a preacher.

You can be the greatest bridge to God for your child. Or, you can become the greatest barrier to you child reaching God.

We have had parents "ground" their teens from going to a youth group because of misbehavior. How foolish that can be! Why would a parent keep a child away from God's presence when he or she misbehaves? Just the opposite should be the case. Whenever a child is misbehaving, get that child into worship, God's presence, and with other godly friends as much as possible!

I want to be certain that my words, attitudes or actions don't cause my child to stumble in their pursuit of God.

I do desire that my fiery passion for God would ignite their fire for Him.

I want my faults and sins to be confessed and removed so that I become a path to the Father for my child not a dead end to my child's pursuit of God.

I desire to be a green light not a red light in my child's spiritual journey.

Our desire for our child needs to such a powerful spiritual and material inheritance and legacy that they do greater works in the Kingdom of God than we ever did. I want them to have more signs and wonders follow them than I ever experienced. I desire for their service to others to far exceed anything I did or could ever have imagined.

If you are in your child's way to God, humble yourself as Christ did. Instead of being "in the way" get out of the way so that your child is encouraged and helped to the Father by your life.

Let this mind be in you which was also in Christ Jesus, who, being in the form of God, did not consider it robbery to be equal with God, but made Himself of no reputation, taking the form of a bondservant, and coming in the likeness of men. And being found in appearance as a man, He humbled Himself and became obedient to the point of death, even the death of the cross. (Phil. 2:5-8)

Action Steps I/We Need to Take

_____

_____

_____

_____

_____

_____

_____

_____

_____

_____

#41
Getting a child's respect requires giving respect.

"My child never shows me any respect," complained the mother.

We get what we sow. Sow mercy...receive mercy. Sow kindness...receive kindness. Sow respect...receive respect.

We treat people the way we wish to be treated. Children have a sense of dignity and self-worth. We show them respect by:

- calling them by blessed names
- refusing to curse them
- speaking to their potential
- affirming them to their faces
- calling forth the gifts within them
- accepting whatever special talents they have
- building them up not tearing them down
- treating them the way we wish to be treated

Children have spiritual giftings just like adults. They can pray, minister and serve others in the name of Jesus just as we can. Respect is a two-way street. Show it to your children and they will return respect to you.

Children are not second-class persons. Some adults treat children like they must be their personal servants. They order them around as if they are slaves. This builds resentment and rebellion in a child.

Value the gifts and worth of your child. See your child as God sees him or her.

Then little children were brought to Him that He might put His hands on them and pray, but the disciples rebuked them. But Jesus said, "Let the little children come to Me, and do not forbid them; for of such is the kingdom of heaven." (Matt. 19:13-15)

#42
The goal of healthy families is interdependence not independence or dependence.

"I can't wait until my daughter is independent and moves out," shared a mother.

Some parents live for the day when their child leaves home. Such parents are destined to be lonely in their old age. We are not raising children to be isolated islands in the sea of humanity.

A spirit of independence has so permeated many family that everyone does *what is right in his own eyes*. This leads to selfishness and brokenness in families.

Imagine three circles representing the family:

Independence—In this circle, everyone is facing outward, away from the middle. No one is holding hands. No face engages another face. No connection is made. Slowly each person moves one step at a time away from the circle. Finally, there is no circle at all. Only isolated individuals exist lost in a sea of humanity.

Dependence—In this circle, everyone is leaning on one person in the center of the circle. This person is trying to hold up the rest of the circle. The load is heavy on one and non-existent for the others. If that one person on whom everyone depends falls, they all fall. Everyone's life revolves around the controlling person in the middle.

Interdependence—In this circle, everyone is facing in and hold hands. Everyone can see the others and can freely connect with everyone else. All have their individual identity but they all need and appreciate one another.

Interdependent families help one another throughout life. They are friends for life. They walk through life supporting, affirming and helping one another. If one stumbles the others help pick him up. If one excels, the others rejoice. Families are like a miniature church. Each family member is a part of the whole, important to the whole, and connected to the whole family.

The members should have the same care for one another. And if one member suffers, all the members suffer with it; or if one member is honored, all the members rejoice with it. Now you are the body of Christ, and members individually. (1 Cor. 12:25-27)

Action Steps I/We Need to Take

_____

_____

_____

_____

_____

_____

_____

_____

_____

_____

_____

#43
Healthy boundaries protect parents and children.

"We never seem to have any privacy," complained the parents.

These parents had failed to set healthy boundaries to protect themselves and also protect their children. Their problem centered around the bedroom. As small children, their children had been permitted to sleep with their parents and come in and out of their bedroom without permission. The children were allowed to go through their parents' closets and drawers. They took whatever money they saw laying around in the bedroom.

As the children grew older, the parents regretted their lack of privacy and intimacy. They had failed to create healthy boundaries around their bedroom. The same principle can be applied to other areas of family living.

Boundaries are not walls. They are simply private spaces which protect a person from invasion and abuse. What boundaries have you set to protect yourself and your children?

Within healthy boundaries exist blessings. For example, within the boundaries of using substances, we allowed our children to drink ice tea and coffee but not alcohol or smoke cigarettes. We taught them that outside of these healthy boundaries existed addiction, poor health, and even death. Inside the boundaries of treating our bodies right existed health and life.

Boundaries can focus on dos instead of don'ts. Do eat healthy. Do pray. Do read and memorize the work. Do your homework. Do watch wholesome TV and listen to wholesome music. In order to set these boundaries we must openly examine and discuss our children what is "wholesome" and what is "polluted." What boundaries exist in your family for morality, privacy, holiness, spiritual discipline, education, TV watching, playing games, using computers, etc.? Discuss boundaries and set them with your children. In doing that, you will teach your children about healthy boundaries.

The law of the LORD is perfect, converting the soul; The testimony of the LORD is sure, making wise the simple; The statutes of the LORD are right, rejoicing the heart; The commandment of the LORD is pure, enlightening the eyes; Moreover by them Your servant is warned, And in keeping them there is great reward. (Ps. 19:7-8, 11)

Action Steps I/We Need to Take

_____

_____

_____

_____

_____

_____

_____

_____

_____

_____

#44
With increased responsibility comes increased privilege.

"Everything you enjoy is a privilege not a right," explained the wise parent.

A right is something I have believe I deserve. But a privilege is a gift I have shown that I can handle responsibly. Everything I receive is a gift. I am a steward not an owner.

For example, my room is not a right but a privilege. My allowance, clothes, outings and games are not a right but a privilege. These are attitudes that children must develop. They learn them from parents.

As a child matures and can responsibly handle more privilege, more opportunity is given by the parent for that child to make right decisions.

For example, as my child takes more responsibility for the cleaning and care of his clothes, then he has more privileges in shopping for and selecting his clothes.

As my child takes responsibility for doing chores around the house—just as the parents share in the chores, then the child has more privileges in using what's in the house like the TV, computer, phone, etc. From an early age, a child is taught to be a steward not a consumer.

Consumers have the attitude that they own what they buy. Stewards know that everything they have for the moment belongs to God. Are you raising your children to be stewards or consumers?

Children who are consumers focus on *their* rights, possessions and materialism. Children who become stewards develop an attitude of gratitude and appreciate the privilege of managing that which belongs to another—God.

Well done, good and faithful servant; you were faithful
over a few things, I will make you ruler over many things.
Enter into the joy of your lord. (Matt. 25:21-22)

#45
Divorce breaks both the hearts of God and children.

"I can't understand why my child is so upset with me all of the time," complained a divorced father.

I wish I had taped all the conversations I have had through the years with the children of divorced parents. Before any parents ever contemplated a divorce, I would have them listen to the hurt and pain in the lives of the victims of divorce—children.

God hates divorce. We work closely with a godly, restored couple both of whom have been divorced and are in their second marriage. God has forgiven and restored both of them and their ex-spouses, but the scars of divorce forever carry the pain and consequences of brokenness. They can relate from personal experience the pain of divorce to other couples

Most alienated husbands and wives can work through their problems if both repent, both forgive, both learn new ways of relating and both are willing to change. Marriage is a covenant among three persons—husband, wife and God. A threefold cord is not easily broken.

For a brief time in our marriage, my wife and I allowed ourselves both to speak and think the divorce word. We were even counseled by some to get a divorce. But God's covenant was more important than our selfish desires. We wanted to be happy. We discovered that true joy came when we began to want our spouse's happiness above our own.

Make a vow today. Vow never to use the "d" (divorce) word in your marriage. Decide that you will do whatever it takes to work through your problems with the help of the Lord and others.

And this is the second thing you do: You cover the altar of the Lord with tears, With weeping and crying; so He does not regard the offering anymore, nor receive it with goodwill from your hands. Yet you say, "For what reason?" Because the Lord has been witness Between you and the wife of your youth, with whom you have dealt treacherously; Yet she is your companion and your wife by covenant. But did He not make them one, having a remnant of the Spirit? And why one? he seeks godly offspring. Therefore take heed to your spirit, and let none deal treacherously with the wife of his youth. (Mal. 2:13-15)

Action Steps I/We Need to Take

_____

_____

_____

_____

_____

_____

_____

_____

_____

_____

#46
It's not about you...it's about
your seed and your seed's seed.

"Look at the shame you caused me," moaned the parent to a rebellious child.

It's not about you. Parenting focuses on what God wants us to say and do with our children. Parenting is about training up children in the ways of the Lord.

Parenting is not about our wants...our convenience...our happiness...or pleasing ourselves.

Children are a gift from God. We are stewards not owners. They are not our possession.

As such, it's essential that we recognize that successful parenting is not about how good we look. Too many parents believe their good name is at stake in the behavior of their children. They want their children to succeed so that they, as parents, will look good to their peers.

But, it's not about our reputation. It's about His. God's name is at sake in our seed and our seed's seed. As we read in Malachi 2:14, the Lord is looking for godly seed. We invest blessing in our children so that they will have an inheritance that overflows into the lives of their children and their children's children.

There is no success without a successor. There is no inheritance without an heir. There is no legacy without one who will take the legacy forward into the future.

What seed are you sowing into your seed so that they can bear fruit and sow seed into their seed?

What spiritual, emotional, intellectual and material inheritance are you leaving for your children?

When a good man dies, he leaves an inheritance
to his grandchildren. (Prov. 13:22 TLB)

#47
Give your children to God and you'll always have them.

"I hope I never lose my children," said a controlling mother.

She lived her life through her children. When they left home and started families of their own, this lonely mother lost her reason to live. She had lived her life through her children.

Possess children only to lose them. Children belong to God not to parents, society or the government.

The mother and father of a teenager had to finally surrender the discipline and control of their son to God. They gave up trying to manage his life. The discipline of the Father was harsher than theirs and also more effective.

The loving father in Luke 15 allowed his son to leave and go to a faraway country. He never stopped believing that son would come home and restore the relationship. But he had to let go and let God take control. And when the son *came to himself*, he returned to the loving father.

You may have a child in the foreign land of rebellion and estrangement right now. Consider the parable in Luke 15 as your source of hope:

- Your child is never too wicked. *The prodigal son wished his father dead and demanded his inheritance.*
- Your child is never too far away. *The prodigal son went to a faraway land.*
- Your child is never too lost. *The penniless, Jewish boy was tending unclean pigs—what degradation!*
- Your child is never absent too long. *The loving Father waited, looking down the road until that day the son finally came to himself.*

The loving parent is willing to let a child run straight into the discipline of the Father. Let the child go. The loving parent is also always ready *to let God do whatever it takes; wait for as long as* it takes, *to forgive; to take back; to restore;* and *to celebrate a child's return with blessing*...not with "I told you so."

"For my son was dead is alive again; He was lost and is found."
And they began to be merry. (Luke 15:24)

Action Steps I/We Need to Take

_____

_____

_____

_____

_____

_____

_____

_____

_____

_____

_____

#48
Purpose speaks to a child's potential; identity speaks to a child's destiny.

"God never starts anything He hasn't already finished," taught Myles Monroe.

How true. God instills purpose in all He creates. Your child was created with meaning and purpose. The good work He began in your child, God will see through to completion.

We must imitate God's way of parenting. Everything we say, teach and do with our child must be on-purpose. We are raising a child in the fear of the Lord. If our words and actions point to the Father, we are on purpose. If they point to anything else, we are off-purpose.

The purpose within a child is always unfolding. It is never fully realized until that child comes to face to face with Jesus at Christ's seat of judgment.

A purpose is not a goal or an objective. We continually realized objective and reach goals as we journey toward our purpose in life. Ultimately, we all have the ultimate purpose of being "in Christ" and of "worshipping and serving God." Jesus said, "You shall worship the LORD your God, and Him only you shall serve" (Matt. 4:10).

Identity reveals destiny. One of the key questions your child will ask is, "Who am I?" He will discover the answer to that question, when he finally asks, "Whose am I?" The identity crisis of every child is resolved when they receive Jesus Christ as Lord and Savior. Jesus reveals that we "belong to Christ" (Mark 9:41).

When a child's identity is "in Christ," then that child knows his destiny—to rule and reign on high with Him!

> *For You were slain, And have redeemed us to God by Your blood Out of every tribe and tongue and people and nation, And have made us kings and priests to our God; And we shall reign on the earth."* (Rev. 5:9-10)

#49
Promise-keeping builds trust on both sides of the fence.

"Dad never keeps his promises," complained the young boy.

For this child, the path of his life was littered with the broken glass of shattered promises. His dad was always promising to do something with him but rarely keeping his promises. Expectantly the son would wait at the door for his father to come home and play with him, take him out, or spend time with him as he promised. But almost always the father had just another meeting, another call or another trip.

The father would always ask for forgiveness and make another promise. The son forgave but soon lost trust in his father's words.

What about you? Are you a promise-keeper or a promise-breaker? A promise-keeper says what he means and does it. A promise-keeper puts priority on family relationships. A promise-keeper believes that his word is his bond.

This same father became very upset when his son as a teenager began to break his promises. The son promised to come in on time but never did. The son promised to study hard but didn't. The son promised to remain a virgin, but couldn't.

Promise-keeping works both ways. But it starts with the parent.

What promises have you made? What promises need to be kept? What repentance needs to be offered to your child?

But let your 'Yes' be 'Yes,' and your 'No,' 'No.' (Matt. 5:37)

For all the promises of God in Him are Yes, and in Him. Amen, to the glory of God through us. (2 Cor. 1:20)

#50
In a child's mind: A car—$$$; A computer—$$;
A designer item—$; You—Priceless!

I saw this TV ad for MasterCard. It named off all the things that MasterCard could buy and then it listed what MasterCard could not buy because that experience was priceless.

Children love for us to buy them things. But we cannot buy love. We cannot buy any substitutes for our presence, our time, and our love.

Children want us not just our money and provision.

If you are trying to buy your child's love or if you feel guilty about not being with your child and assuage your guilt with buying stuff, then you are loving stuff and using your family instead of loving your family and using stuff.

Your child doesn't need stuff; he needs you.

So, what are you giving your child? Summarize the last three days and write down the amount of time you have spent with your child(ren).

Day 1: _____

Day 2: _____

Day 3: _____

Now ask the Father: Am I spending enough time with my child so that what he really gets is me and not stuff?

And these words which I command you today shall be in your heart. You shall teach them diligently to your children, and shall talk of them when you sit in your house, when you walk by the way, when you lie down, and when you rise up. You shall bind them as a sign on your hand, and they shall be as frontlets between your eyes. You shall write them on the doorposts of your house and on your gates. (Deut. 6:6-9)

#51

Who children are is far more important than what they do. Children are human beings not human doings.

Some parents constantly are telling children "Do this" or "Don't do this." Life is filled with dos and don'ts.

But a child's self-esteem isn't founded on performance; it's rooted in being. Who we are is far more important than what we do.

- Help your child mature by emphasizing who he or she is. Tell a child, "You are..."
- Fearfully and wonderfully made by God.
- Full of potential and promise.
- Capable of doing anything through Christ who strengthens you.
- Loved and accepted by both God and me.
- Talented and gifted.
- Intelligent and sensitive.
- Special and unique.
- Loving and kind.

This isn't a complete list. You need to complete it. It's just to get you started. Make a list now for your child. Begin to focus on who your child is in Christ Jesus not what they can do. You are...

1. _____

2. _____

3. _____

4. _____

5. _____

But you are a chosen generation, a royal priesthood, a holy nation, His own special people, that you may proclaim the praises of Him who called you out of darkness into His marvelous light; who once were not a people but are now the people of God, who had not obtained mercy but now have obtained mercy. (1 Peter 2:9-10)

Action Steps I/We Need to Take

_____

_____

_____

_____

_____

_____

_____

_____

_____

_____

#52

Unconditional love says, "There is nothing you can do that will make me stop loving you."

Are you willing to love your child unconditionally? That means that you love doesn't depend on what they do. Your love for you child isn't withdrawn just because you are upset with their behavior or attitude.

Conditional love is a controlling, manipulative love. It says, "I will love you if...." God's love (agape) says, "I will love you always."

Unconditional love seeks the child's best. It is a selfless, expecting-nothing-in-return loving. When we love to get something in return we are manipulating and trying to control a child.

Unconditional love is patient. It spends whatever time is necessary to reach out to a child. It believes in the child and God's potential for that child. Unconditional love never quits or gives up.

Unconditional love rejoices in the successes of a child and encourages and child when he stumbles or makes a mistake. Love refuses to believe that mistakes make a child a failure.

Unconditional love isn't easily angered and doesn't provoke children to anger. It's not oversensitive or overreacting.

Unconditional love rejoices in the truth and speaks the truth loving to the child.

Unconditional love endures hardship, rejection, pain and discouragement. No matter what a child does to the parent, the parent continues to love and encourage the child.

Are you willing to say to your child, "There is nothing you can do to make me stop loving you!"

Love suffers long and is kind; love does not envy; love does not parade itself, is not puffed up; does not behave rudely, does not seek its own, is not provoked, thinks no evil; does not rejoice in iniquity, but rejoices in the truth; bears all things, believes all things, hopes all things, endures all things. Love never fails. (1 Cor. 13:4-8)

#53

Right reactions arise from acting like God not just acting like our parents.

"God squeezes us to see what will come out," the speaker commented.

When you squeeze a tube of toothpaste, you expect toothpaste to come out. When you squeeze a parent, what do you expect to come out?

Obviously whatever is in us will come out especially when we are under stress and pressure. Too often, the old habits and ways of our parents come out when we react to misbehaving children.

The only way to change is to allow God to change us. In order to break with old parenting habits and destructive comments is to be changed by the power of God.

One of the most effective ways to cut of the past and become a *new parent in Christ Jesus* is to pray. Pray changes us.

The ineffective way to pray is, *God change my child!*

The effective way to pray is, *God change me.*

When you ask God to change you, He empowers you to break old parenting habits and to begin implementing the new. When God changes you, you will begin acting and reacting more and more like Him.

Therefore, if anyone is in Christ, he is a new creation; old things have passed away; behold, all things have become new. (2 Cor. 5:17)

#54

No substitute exists for quality, one-on-one time with children.

"I just don't have enough time to spend quality time with my child," bemoaned the parent.

Then find the time! Children need their parents around. We find time for everything else—work, rest, hobbies, talking on the phone, watching TV, entertainment, eating, etc.

We give our time to what's important to us. Our priorities must be:

God first.
Family second.
Church and work next.
Then all the rest.

Jesus reminds us that there is no greater love than laying down one's life for a friend. "Greater love has no one than this, than to lay down one's life for his friends" (John 15:13).

What are you dying for? The moment you are born, you start dying. Every minute that passes by, you have died to that parent of your life. Realistically, spending our time means dying for that person or thing we spend our time doing. For some parents, what they're dying to is their jobs. But where will the boss or colleagues be when they are old and lonely?

When your life is in it's twilight years your true friends will still be around. True friends will be those you have invested your time in.

Will your children be your true friends in your old age?

Children need us. We need to be there for them when they play their sports, receive their awards, need help with their homework and struggle with tough decisions in life. Children need us there when they worship, pray and study God's Word.

Are you *there* for your children? The only way to truly *be there* for your child is to spend one-on-one time with your child. The average father or mother spends less than 15 minutes a day with a child. Some parents spend more time walking a dog, putting on makeup or getting dressed than talking with and sharing with children. What about you? How much time daily will you give to your child?

I covenant with God and my child to average at least _____ a day together.

Greater love has no one than this, than to lay down one's life for his friends. (John 15:13)

Action Steps I/We Need to Take

_____

_____

_____

_____

_____

_____

_____

_____

_____

_____

#55

Your relationship with your child is often more important than your being right.

Do you have to always be right even if means sacrificing your relationship with a child?

Winning arguments with our child is not the way to resolve conflict. Discipline teaches what's right. That's different than having to "be right."

I may believe what's right but how I communicate and act toward a child can be completely wrong. The old adage has some validity here: *it's not what you say but how you say it.*

Children are not the enemy. You are not in a war against a child. We do not battle against flesh and blood. We war against the true enemy of our souls—Satan.

You can be right, win the argument and defeat the child. But what have you accomplished? The child is not wounded, crushed, hurt, and angry. This leads to offense and bitterness, feelings of rejection and a breaking of relationship.

Yes, parents must speak the truth *in love.* In order to be right, I don't have to prove my child wrong and win the argument. I do have to teach truth, love unconditionally, and often wait for a child to understand what's right. Instant victories can lead to long-term hurt and brokenness.

The next time you feel the urge to steamroll over your child's feelings, step back. Be quick to listen. Slow to speak and especially slow to anger. Also remember that the next statement you make to a child will either speak life or death. There's something more important than being right. It's being in a loving, forgiving and lasting relationship with your child.

Speaking the truth in love. (Eph. 4:15)

#56
Replace criticism with affirmation.

"Dad, the only time you ever talk to me is to point out my mistakes," complained the son.

Make a journal. Log how many times a day you say something negative to your child. Then log all the positive, affirming and encouraging things you say daily to your child. Which list is longer?

We often get into the bad habit of pointing out all the things wrong with our children but failing to affirm them when they show responsibility and a healthy attitude.

Replace criticism with kind correction and teaching. Find ways to say to your child...

"I thank God for _____."

"I appreciate you when _____."

"I am proud of you because _____."

"You are special to me."

"I love you."

"Will you pray for me today about _____."

"I want to thank you for _____."

Positive affirmation makes deposits into the emotional bank of your child. Criticism makes withdrawals. Children grow and mature when they have a positive balance in their emotional bank account. But they become critical and cynical, rebellious and angry, when they must carry a negative balance.

Have you made any deposits lately? Is your child's emotional bank account overflowing or overdrawn?

Therefore encourage one another and build each other up,
just as in fact you are doing. (1 Thess. 5:11)

#57
Building on a child's strengths helps him/her overcome weaknesses.

Imagine a roof with a rotten support beam. Now you have two choices:

1.   Tear out the beam to replace it and risk having the roof fall in on you.
2.   Or, put in a new beam and then tear out the old.

Continuing attacking a child's weaknesses risks destroying the child. Building on a child's strengths will...

*   Help a child overcome weakness
*   Affirm and encourage a child
*   Build trust between you and the child
*   Teach a child lasting truths
*   Communicate your love and care
*   Construct character in your child
*   Lead to long-term growth and maturity
*   Strengthen your relationship with your child

Think of it another way. If you always tell a child what not to do, they will never learn what to do. Focusing on what's wrong doesn't teach what's right.

Jesus reminds us that we can empty a house of demons, but if it remains empty, only more demons will come back to fill it. We can empty a child of weakness but if no strength has been built, the weaknesses will only return.

Building on strength is edification. Find ways to edify your child today!

Therefore let us pursue the things which make for peace and the things by which one may edify another. (Rom. 14:19)

#58
Intimidation a child creates a fearful, angry adult.

"You will obey me or I will beat you until the sun don't shine," yelled the angry parent.

Instill the fear of us in a child sows seeds of destruction into our relationship.

Intimidation tries to control a child by fear. A child learns to fear the parent and obeys the parent fearing emotional or physical pain—which is usually abusive.

Physical intimidation uses beating.

Emotional intimidation uses angry, tearing, degrading, undignified words and actions.

Mental intimidation plays mind games with a child and tries to make a child look dumb or ignorant.

Spiritual intimidation uses the Bible as a legal whip and pictures God as an angry, wrathful, judging tyrant.

All intimidation is abusive.

If you intimidate your child or anyone else in your family, get help. Go to a pastor, counselor, or helping professional. You are a danger to yourself and others.

Out of fear, a child may obey an intimidating parent outwardly, but inwardly that child will become rebellious and mean. That child will learn to intimidate others and will grow up into an abusive parent.

For God has not given us a spirit of fear, but of power
and of love and of a sound mind. (2 Tim. 1:7)

#59
Domination a child creates a weak, immature adult.

Domination seeks to control a child's thoughts, emotions, behaviors and will.

The parent who feels it's necessary to control a child is insecure. Feeling inwardly inadequate, a controlling parent outwardly appears to be strong, dominating, aggressive and overly confident.

Dominating a child results in a child who fails to mature. Domination creates dependent children who can never make their own decisions. Or, domination creates rebellious children who try to leave home as soon as possible.

Domination says....
- Think what I think
- Do what I do
- Be what I am
- Feel what I feel
- Breathe when I breathe

The controlling parent is always worried about what a child is thinking or doing. The dominating parent cannot trust a child.

If you are dominating your child, surrender control to God. Take responsibility for your own feelings and actions, and let go of responsibility for everyone else's.

I beseech you therefore, brethren, by the mercies of God, that you present your bodies a living sacrifice, holy, acceptable to God, which is your reasonable service. And do not be conformed to this world, but be transformed by the renewing of your mind, that you may prove what is that good and acceptable and perfect will of God. (Rom. 12:1-2)

#60
Manipulation a child creates a distrusting, controlling adult.

Manipulation seeks to get a child to do what's best for us instead of what's best for them.

Manipulation uses bribes, false promises, lies and deceit to get our way.

We manipulate children fearing that if they make decisions on their own that they will make wrong decisions. But there are times when a child will fail. They will learn from failure just as we have.

We cannot manipulate children or circumstances to get our way. Doing so will create children who will not be able to trust us or others. They will grow up into distrusting and controlling adults.

We manipulate so that we can get the agreement or the approval of others. We manipulate because we believe we must win at any cost.

Instead of manipulating your child, release your child to be creative, curious, inventive and exploring. Teach your child the truth. Equip your child how to make right from wrong decisions. Trust your child to make more and more of his or her own decisions. When they make a wrong decision, help them correct the mistake and learn from it.

Set your child free to grow into a trusting adult.

Now the Lord is the Spirit; and where the
Spirit of the Lord is, there is liberty. (2 Cor. 3:17)

#61
Forgiveness heals a child's hurts.

"If you do that, I don't think I will ever be able to forgive you," threatened the parent.

Forgiveness is never an option; it's a must. Jesus commands us to forgive. If we don't forgive, our Father in heaven will not forgive us (Matt. 6).

Forgiveness brings healing a restoration into a child's life. At times, our actions communicate unforgiveness to a child. Here are some unforgiving behaviors we should avoid:

- The silent treatment
- Withdrawing love or emotional closeness from a child
- Constantly bringing up a child's past failures and mistakes
- Becoming offended with a child
- Criticizing our children
- Belittling our children in front of others
- Saying that we forgive but not meaning it

Forgiveness means letting go of the past. We refuse to "go fishing" into the past mistakes and failures of our child. We genuinely forgive and forget.

Be willing to forgive often. Children need lots of forgiveness.

Also, be willing to ask for forgiveness when you make a mistake. Put these words into your vocabulary. "Will you forgive me?"

Then Peter came to Him and said, "Lord, how often shall my brother sin against me, and I forgive him? Up to seven times?" Jesus said to him, "I do not say to you, up to seven times, but up to seventy times seven (Matt. 18:21-22)

#62
Speak to a child's heart not only about their behavior. Know your child's love languages.

Gary Chapman wrote a wonderful book on our five love languages. Learn your child's expressive and receptive love languages.

Our expressive love language is the one with which we prefer to show love to other.

Our receptive love language is the one from which we like to receive love from others. Here are the five languages of love:

1. **Quality time.** This is spending meaningful and sufficient time one on one with a child.
2. **Gift giving.** Gifts no matter what the price are expressions of love.
3. **Acts of service.** These are acts that another person needs and doesn't have to ask for in order to receive them.
4. **Affirming words.** Kind, uplifting and encouraging expressions of love are needed daily.
5. **Physical touch.** It may be anything from rumbling on the floor and play wrestling with a child to hugs, kisses, and loving pats.

Take time to learn which love language your child prefers to express love in and which one they like to receive. While we may enjoy all expressions of love, we usually prefer one or two over the others.

If your expressive love language is gift giving, but your child prefers receiving love in quality time, you can give them all the gifts in the world and they won't feel love.

Sit down and talk over this list with your children. Let them tell you about their love languages and you share with them about your preference.

Love is the fulfillment of the law. (Rom. 13:10)

#63
Parenting for life is a given; friends for life is hard work.

We're always a parent. But becoming our child's friend takes hard work.

Our adult children and their spouses are among our best friends. We cherish our time with them. But it takes hard work, lots of time and talking, and continual forgiveness and understanding.

Working on friendship can include these:
- Talking daily on the phone
- Praying together
- Going out to eat together
- Sharing meals together
- Talking about important issues
- Reading books together
- Helping with finances
- Watching the grandchildren
- Going on trips together
- Expressing love in the five love languages

You get the idea. Now add to the list. Talk it over with you children. Make a plan to continually bless and befriend your children no matter how old your or they become.

A friend loves at all times. (Prov. 17:17)

#64
The door of tough love must open both ways.

My teenage daughter and I had a long talk. She had been in a state of increasing rebellion for over two years. Now she was sneaking out in the middle of the night to be with her friends. Our relationship was strained to the maximum.

So, we were on a long walk having a long talk. I shared my feelings and she shared hers.

Then I made a statement I never imagined I would have to make, "Either you will accept us as your parents and obey us or you will have to move out."

She looked at me in disbelief and then started crying. My love had to be tough for her sake. Her behavior was destroying both her and our family. I love and believed in her but I knew that a line had to be drawn in the sand.

We reconciled with tears and forgiveness. At times, separation is the only path back to restoration. The rift becomes so deep that a child must experience the consequences of their behavior in order to return back to what's right.

The separation doesn't mean that the door back home is closed and locked. It simply means that repentance, forgiveness, and restoration.

The door is always open and the light is always for your return, we say to our children in touch love. The door of tough love always swings out if they must leave and in for their return.

And the younger of them said to his father, 'Father, give me the portion of goods that falls to me.' So he divided to them his livelihood. And not many days after, the younger son gathered all together, journeyed to a far country, and there wasted his possessions with prodigal living. (Luke 15:12-14)

#65
Forgive your child before he or she repents.

Proactive forgiveness is...
- Deciding that forgiveness is a must not an option
- Announcing to your children that forgiveness will always be real in your relationship.
- Also announcing to your children the consequences for their disobedience.
- Never cheap grace.
- Always ready to reach out.
- Never waiting for the child to repent first.
- Always ready to correct and teach.
- Never condemning or critical.
- Always filled with patience and understanding.
- Never mindful of past mistakes.
- Always expecting new and positive change in us and our children.

Always ready to forgive doesn't mean you're permissive. It does mean you are like the Father.

Your heavenly Father will forgive you if you forgive
those who sin against you; but if you refuse to forgive
them, he will not forgive you. (Matt. 6:14) TLB

#66
Don't waste your tears; save them for a river of intercession and prayer.

"I just don't know where I went wrong." the young mother said. "Billy is defiant, and won't obey me at all." Weeping bitterly, she sank into the chair and buried her face in her hands.

My heart went out to this mother whose heart was so obviously broken. She blamed herself for the things her son did and seemed helpless to stop him.

Crying out like this mother are countless thousands of other mothers and fathers around the globe. They wonder where they went wrong or what they could have done differently. Each situation is different, though there are often similarities like...

- Not establishing boundaries
- Intermittent follow through with discipline
- Unreasoned responses to minor infractions of the rules
- Rules that changed as the parents mood changed

It's time for this young mother and other parents like her to stop crying the day away and instead begin interceding for their child before God. So long as parents throw up their hands in surrender, crying will not help. However, crying out to God to shape and mold the child avails much.

It's not enough to just be sorry for past failures. Become proactive in your prayers—it's never too late see God move.

The effective, fervent prayer of a righteous man avails much. Elijah was a man with a nature like ours, and he prayed earnestly that it would not rain; and it did not rain on the land for three years and six months. And he prayed again, and the heaven gave rain, and the earth produced its fruit. (James 5:16b-18)

#67

A name of blessing is spoken daily over a child; a misnamed child lives with a daily curse.

What's in a name? You may be surprised at the answer to this question, because a child's identity is closely tied to the name you've given him.

Throughout Scripture, we see the importance of names. In fact, Jesus renamed Simon, and Saul of Tarsus took on another form of his name.

Though we think a name is mute and without power, we're wrong. Scripture says that when we receive our final reward, we'll be given a new name that no other person has ever had.

Words are powerful, and names are spoken with words. Jabez was a man of honor in the Old Testament, and God honored him. However, his name means "because I bore him in pain."

Imagine that every time you heard your name you were reminded of the pain you caused your mother. No wonder he prayed that he would not cause pain (1 Chron. 4:9-10).

Jesus was called Immanuel by the angels who heralded His birth. Immanuel means, "God with us."

Those who have received Jesus are called Christians or Christ ones. What name will you call your child? Will it be a name of blessing or a name that brings curse?

And she [Leah] conceived again and bore a son, and said, "Now I will praise the LORD." Therefore she called his name Judah. (Gen. 29:35)

#68

Transgressing the Ten Commandments creates generational curses; obeying them creates endless blessing.

"The Ten Commandments aren't relevant any longer. We're under grace, not the Law."

This tragic misunderstanding is prevalent throughout the church. However, we must understand that the Law has never been replaced it's just been fulfilled in Jesus.

Jesus said that the Law and Prophets were captured in two commands: Love the Lord with all your heart, might, mind, and strength, and love your neighbor as you love yourself. So now we live under the Law of Love.

However, breaking the Commandments still brings forth a curse because you've moved outside the Law of Love.

Teach your child to obey the Ten Commandments because they will educate her in how to live. Having a consciousness of the Law ensures the child will be more careful in her dealings with others and with God. Having no consciousness of the Law means the child will live a rebellious and lawless life.

Teach you child to embrace the Law of Love. As he does, he'll learn what it means to walk closeness with God. Your child can love because God first loved him. You show him the love of God by the close interaction you have with him.

Teach your child how to love—then she will not have to be concerned with the curse.

I call heaven and earth as witnesses today against you, that
I have set before you life and death, blessing and cursing;
therefore choose life, that both you and your descendants may
live; that you may love the LORD your God, that you may
obey His voice, and that you may cling to Him, for He is
your life and the length of your days.... (Deut. 30:19-20)

#69
The best way to teach prayer is to pray over, often and out loud with children.

How often do you pray over your children?

This question convicts many parents because they rarely or never pray over their child. Or, if they do pray, it's after the child is in bed and asleep. Worse, they may only pray when the child is in danger or trouble of some sort.

Your child needs to hear you pray to the Father about them, for them, and over them. They need to hear that you are asking the Lord to bless them and to help them grow up strong and blessed with the abundance of heaven.

When you pray out loud over your child, you are sending them a message of their eternal importance. You express to them that not only are you interested in their success, but God is too.

Praying often teaches the child good habits of prayer. This is something to do proactively, not reactively. By staying in an attitude of prayer, both you and the child are prepared for life's ups and downs.

So how do you pray? Start with a prayer of blessing like the one below inserting their name. Don't be shy, be glad, instead, that God, and your child will listen.

The LORD bless you and keep [name]; The LORD make His face shine upon [name], And be gracious to [name]; The LORD lift up His countenance upon [name], And give [name] peace. (Num 6:24-26)

#70
Teach a child to manage money not credit.

"My kid has a MasterCard with a $10,000 credit limit!" boasted the proud father. What this deluded father didn't realize was that he was bragging about his child having a curse.

We wouldn't boast about our child having an addiction like drugs or pornography, so why would we boast about them being cursed with debt?

Being cursed with debt means that our child is a slave to another master besides God. Debtors determine how much or how little the child must work to pay off the debt.

The focus becomes getting money to pay the debt instead of using money to bless others.

The Bible clearly teaches that we are to be lenders, not borrowers. Therefore, we must teach our children how to manage money so they have it to lend.

Today's market economy says to gather up as much credit you can and live to the max in every area. After all, you can pay for today's pleasure at reduced interest for the first six months. What they don't say is that when you fall into that trap, you stand in danger of paying for life's pleasures for life.

How do you handle money? Are you living an example that you want you child to emulate?

For the LORD your God will bless you just as He promised you; you shall lend to many nations, but you shall not borrow; you shall reign over many nations, but they shall not reign over you. (Deut 15:6)

#71

Leave a spiritual and material inheritance great enough to bless your seed's seed.

Today's message to people is, "Live your life for you. You only go around once."

This self-centered approach to life is deadly to your child. God has given you the means to provide for your family and to bless them beyond your life here on earth.

This is more than leaving a spiritual legacy, it includes a material blessing as well.

Retirement plans enable workers to have enough money for them and their spouse to have a nice life after they stop working. However, many fall short in helping parents plan an inheritance for their children, let alone for their grandchildren.

Parents have a mandate from God to provide for their seed and their seed's seed. It's an honor to bless them, just as our Heavenly Father has blessed us. It also sends a clear message—"You are important."

The message we send to our children when we hoard possessions to ourselves is one of greed and selfishness. Jesus taught clearly that we should desire to give our child the best gifts, just as our Father has given us His best (Luke 11:9-13).

And you shall remember the LORD your God, for it is
He who gives you power to get wealth, that He may
establish His covenant which He swore to your
fathers, as it is this day. (Deut 8:18)

#72

Live to please God and bless ('esher) your children instead of blessing ('esher) God and pleasing your children.

"I just can't seem to make Tiara happy. She's not pleased with anything I do."

Too often, parents seek to please their children instead of pleasing God. It's time to wake up and realize that living to please other people, even your children, is not what life is about.

Live to please God. "How?" you ask. By obeying His commands, not your child's.

Children are basically self-centered. As babies, they cry out for attention to be fed, held, cleaned up, and comforted. They don't know enough to take care of themselves so they depend on you, the parent.

Tragically, many parents continue to live in the "please me" mode of infant rearing when their children are much older. Sadly, these parents live their lives never blessing their seed because they've used everything to try and please them.

Pleasing God means that we will have a balanced approach to blessing our children. The child will be loved beyond measure and valued as a special gift from God, which alone will bless them.

Pleasing God means that parents will leave a spiritual heritage with their child that cannot be taken away. Blessing your children means calling on the One in whom you place your trust to enrich their lives.

Finally, dear brothers and sisters, we urge you in the name of the Lord Jesus to live in a way that pleases God, as we have taught you. You are doing this already, and we encourage you to do so more and more. (1 Thess 4:1 NLT)

#73
Children need to learn that God is their source not you.

Parents are the primary care givers of their children. Because children are raised this way, they have the tendency to think of the parents as their source for everything. Wrong!

God is the source of all things. Teach your child that God provides for you so that you can provide for them. Teac them that even when it comes from your hand, it first came from God.

Teach your children to be good stewards and to thank God for all the ways He has blessed them, even those blessings that have come through you. Teach them that God uses parents, employers, the church, friends, and others as vessels through which to pour out blessings on them.

Your children are to be blessings as well. Teach the child that God will use him or her to bless others through what He has abundantly blessed them.

By focusing their eyes on God and not you, they see His hand of benevolence and provision in all that you do. This promotes a healthy image of God as the One who provides for them.

When your child learns that God is the One who sustains them, their prayers of thanksgiving will take on new meaning. They will truly see God as the Creator and Sustainer of the universe.

Therefore do not worry, saying, 'What shall we eat?' or 'What shall we drink?' or 'What shall we wear?' For after all these things the Gentiles seek. For your heavenly Father knows that you need all these things. But seek first the kingdom of God and His righteousness, and all these things shall be added to you. (Matt 6:31-33)

#74

The fruit of the Spirit in a child grows from the seeds a parent sows.

How fruitful are you? Does the Holy Spirit have the freedom in your life to develop fruit? Are you living your life to please God? What seed have you sown in your children's lives that will grow?

These questions were swirling in my head as I hurried to the airport to catch another plane. I was busy in the ministry, busy in my writing, busy in my relationship building...I was just plain busy. But was I busy doing the right things?

My youngest son caught me up short by asking why I didn't love him. I was astonished at the thought. Of course I loved him. The problem was, I didn't show it in a way that he could relate.

He needed my presence to <u>feel</u> the love I had for him. He couldn't sense it from my while I was hundreds or even thousands of miles away from him. Nor could he get what he needed by me just telling him. It was presence that he craved.

It's the same with God. We teach our children about relationships with God in the same way we teach them about relationships with others. God yearns for our presence, mere words don't cut it.

Do you spend time with God? Do your children know it? Do you teach them what it takes to have a personal relationship with God?

Then Moses said to the LORD, "....Now therefore, I pray, if I have found grace in Your sight, show me now Your way, that I may know You and that I may find grace in Your sight...." (Exodus 33:12-13)

#75
Sow into your children to give them seed not only fruit.

"If you can hold it in your hand, it's your seed, not the harvest." When I first heard that phrase, I was challenged like I had not been in some time.

I began to think of all the times I held in my hands what I thought was the harvest and wondered why it didn't go very far. Now I knew why—it was my seed.

Think about your children. What have you sown into their lives? Have you sown abundantly so that when the harvest comes they will have seed of their own to plant?

What are you sowing?

- Anger
- Resentment
- Love
- Charity
- Finances
- Greed
- Blessing
- Cursing

What you sow into their lives you will reap—not only you but they as well. What legacy are you going to leave in their life?

I encourage you to sow love, charity, blessing, material wealth, integrity, faithfulness, and mercy. These will bring an abundant harvest that will last them a lifetime.

Begin today to sow generously in your child. I promise that the harvest will be great and will continue long past your wildest dreams.

But this I say: He who sows sparingly will also reap sparingly, and he who sows bountifully will also reap bountifully. So let each one give as he purposes in his heart, not grudgingly or of necessity; for God loves a cheerful giver. And God is able to make all grace abound toward you, that you, always having all sufficiency in all things, may have an abundance for every good work. (2 Cor. 9:6-8)

Action Steps I/We Need to Take

_____

_____

_____

_____

_____

_____

_____

_____

_____

_____

#76
The future of children is not determined by their past but rather God's plan.

"You'll never amount to anything." "You never finish what you start." "Why are you a quitter?"

These statements seek to rob the destiny that God has for your child. Blanket statements that seek to place a false identity on them choke out the air of God's plan and can cause them to suffocate and be just what you've called them to be.

Look at your own past. Were you the model child growing up? Did you always make the right choices? Did you ever make any mistakes in what you did?

Of course you made mistakes, we all do. However, did your past keep you from God's love and concern? Did your past prevent God from doing a mighty work in you?

Remember this: Your child is a person with a soul just like you. God is vitally interested in them just as He is vitally interested in you.

Your child's past is not part of their future. That's what the enemy wants them to think, so don't you enter into agreement with him! Instead, show your child that God's plan is what's important for them to take hold of.

God will never let a person's past dictate their future so long as they have placed their future in His hands. Teach your child to trust God's plan. It's far better than anything you or they could conceive.

Therefore, if anyone is in Christ, he is a new creation;
old things have passed away; behold,
all *things have become new. (2 Cor. 5:17)*

#77
Teach your child to choose blessing each day rather than curse.

This seems like a "no brainer" but it's important to understand that your child has a choice, just like you do.

Every day, your child is faced with choices that will determine whether or not they will walk in God's blessing or not. Remember, if you aren't in His blessing then you're cursed.

This may sound harsh, but it's true. Your child must learn early on to choose the blessing of God by serving only Him. The blessing comes as they keep His commands and worship only Him. The curse comes by disobedience and worship of self or another god.

What commands must we keep? Jesus said it very clearly in Matthew 22 that the commandment is to love. First, love God, then love your neighbor as yourself.

"Teacher, which is the great commandment in the law?" Jesus said to him, "'You shall love the LORD your God with all your heart, with all your soul, and with all your mind.' This is the first and great commandment. And the second is like it: 'You shall love your neighbor as yourself.' On these two commandments hang all the Law and the Prophets." (Matt. 22:36-40 (NKJV)

As we sow love and compassion into our children, they will be equipped to love God and love themselves and their neighbors. By so doing, they will choose blessing and not curse.

Behold, I set before you today a blessing and a curse: the blessing, if you obey the commandments of the LORD your God which I command you today; and the curse, if you do not obey the commandments of the LORD your God, but turn aside from the way which I command you today, to go after other gods which you have not known. (Deut 11:26-28 NKJV)

Other Books by Dr. Larry Keefauver

Proactive Parenting: The Early Years
Inviting God's Presence
Lord I Wish My Husband Would Pray With Me
Lord I Wish My Teenager Would Talk With Me
Lord I Wish My Family Would Get Saved
Hugs for Grandparents
Hugs for Heroes
I'm Praying for You, Friend
I'm Praying for You, Mom
When God Doesn't Heal Now
Experiencing the Holy Spirit
Praying With Smith Wigglesworth
Smith Wigglesworth on Faith
Smith Wigglesworth on Prayer
Smith Wigglesworth on Healing
The 77 Irrefutable Truths of Ministry
The 77 Irrefutable Truths of Prayer
The 77 Irrefutable Truths of Marriage
Healing Words

Conferences & Seminars

Growing Spiritually in Marriage
Parent-Teen Seminars
77 Irrefutable Truths About Parenting
77 Irrefutable Truths About Ministry
A Holy Spirit Encounter
The Presence-Driven Church

For Information or to Order Books:

Dr. Larry Keefauver
P.O. Box 950596
Lake Mary, Fl 32795
1-800-750-5306 • 407-324-5006 (fax)
email: lkeefauv@yahoo.com

Dr. Larry and Judi Keefauver teach parenting seminars around the world. These are the student notes from these seminars.

"Train up (canak) a child in the way he should go, and when he is old he will not turn from it." (Proverbs 22:6)

To train is to _____, _____, _____, _____, _____, _____.

[Example: date syrup] In other words, whatever a child feeds on will train the child. (Deuteronomy 6:4-9; 11:18-21; Psalms 119:11)

Communication

Verbal/Nonverbal
(James 1:19, Proverbs 18:21; John 12:50;
2 Corinthians 8:7; Matthew 12:34-36)

1. Children require _____, talking, truth, trust, togetherness, touch, thanksgiving, time, teaching, Trinity.

2. Answering _____ early saves sorrow later.

3. Speak life not _____ to your children.

4. Only say what the _____ tells you to say; only do what the _____ tells you to do.

5. Talking at children is a _____ with the parent doing all the talking and listening.

6. Want a child to talk? Listen! Willing silence without interruptions primes a child's flow of _____.

7. Your child isn't a garbage can—no _____!

8. Ask your child to share _____ not just opinions.

Discipline

(Ephesians 6:1-4; Hebrews 12:3-11;
Proverbs 1:8; 22:6; Deuteronomy. 6)

9. Discipline corrects and teaches; _____ hurts and crushes.

10. Rules without relationship results in _____.

11. Relationship without rules results in _____.

12. Right behavior reflects right _____.

13. Fearing a parent instills a spirit of deception and deceit; fearing God inspires _____ _____ _____.

14. Contracts mutually agreed upon between parent & child prescribe consequences in _____.

15. _____ must precede penance or change will never happen in your child's behavior or character.

16. Spare the _____; spoil the child. Appropriately applied pain to the butt gets a child's attention and associates wrong with pain instead of pleasure.

17. Because you "say so" doesn't make it so; because
_____ "says so" makes it so.

18. Label behaviors not _____.

19. Discipline allows short-term pain for long-term pleasure; permissiveness allows short-term pleasure for
long-term _____.

Choices

(Joshua24:15; Proverbs 4:20-27)

20. Feelings simply are; _____ to feelings
are right or wrong.

21. Living to make children happy produces _____
families.

22. Be _____ not reactive. Set rules and
consequences in advance. The older the child the
more the child participates in setting boundaries.

Being proactive means equipping your family to:

- Deuteronomy 6:1—Move from curse into blessing.
  Leave Egypt, Cross in Jordan. Shut every door to the
  past; curses; sin habits; bondages
- Deuteronomy 6:4—Hear God. Listen to God's voice in
  His Word, through the Spirit teaching you all truth
- Deuteronomy 6:5—Love with spirit, soul, body
- Deuteronomy 6:6—Obey in your heart
- Deuteronomy 6:7—Impress. Teach diligently, sharpen
  like an arrow; Psalm 127:4

- Deuteronomy 6:7—Talk, communicate, speak friend to friend—all the time; Psalm 35:28; Psalm 8:2; 34:1
- Deuteronomy 6:8—Tie them—hands = actions and work; Bind them —forehead=thoughts; 1 Corinthians 2:16
- Deuteronomy 6:9—Bind them. doors and gates – guard your gateways ; Proverbs 4:13

23. Solving problems for your children never teaches

_____.

24. Answering your child's questions early deposits answers for their late _____ when you're not around.

25. Parental counseling teenagers isn't advice-giving; it's right questions followed by much _____.

HELPING YOUR TEENS SOLVE THEIR OWN PROBLEMS

Understanding Body, Soul and Spirit

Three questions for the Soul...

1. _____

   _____

2. _____

   _____

3. _____

_____

Three questions for the Spirit...

1. _____

2. _____

3. _____

The big questions are:

1. _____

2. _____

3. _____

26. When wrong, go to a child: admit it, quit it,

_____.

27. Teaching right from wrong considers the choice;
    compares to God; chooses the right; and counts the

_____.

THE CRISIS OF TRUTH

Absolute truth is _____

_____

Relativism is _____

_____

Truth is   O_____

               U_____

               C_____

John 8:32 — _____.

Truth is applied _____, _____ and _____.

Principles are the _____.

THE RIGHT FROM WRONG PROCESS (THE 4 C'S)

Step 1. _____

Step 2. _____

Step 3. _____

Step 4. _____

God's way is _____

Our way is _____

Take these actions now:

    1.   _____.

    2.   _____.

    3.   _____.

28. Teaching children _____ empowers them to plan.

29. _____ truth is true for all times, for all place and for all people—parents and children included.

Example

(1 Corinthians 11:1; Philippians 2; Titus 2:6-8; John 13:15)

30. You become an example when your word and way line up with God's word and way.

31. Parental authority is rooted in godly character not role or responsibility.

32. Instilling purpose in children prepares them for trials, tests and tribulation.

33. You're raising adults not _____.

34. _____ will either make you a hypocrite or a hero depending on who a child sees behind your façade.

35. Without church at home, your children will be unwilling to go out to church.

36. Integrity is what you do when you're unaware that you're children are looking and listening.

37. A parent is the first picture of _____ their children see.

38. Teach your children to discern between needs and wants by meeting their needs not their wants.

39. One of the greatest gifts a parent gives a child is

   _____.

40. Quote God not clichés about Him to your children.

41. Get out of your child's way to God. Be a window to God not a mirror of _____.

42. Getting a child's respect requires giving _____.

Family

(Genesis 2:23-25; 1 Corinthians 12; Acts 16:33)

43. The goal of healthy families is interdependence not independence or _____.

44. Healthy _____ protect parents and children.

45. With increased responsibility comes increased

   _____.

46. Divorce breaks both the hearts of God and

   _____.

47. It's not about you...it's about your _____.

48. Give your children to God and you'll always have them. _____ them only to lose them. Children belong to God not to parents, society or the government.

49. Purpose speaks to a child's potential; identity speaks to a child's _____.

50. Promise-keeping builds trust on both sides of the fence.

51. In a child's mind: A car—$$$; A computer—$$; A designer item—$; You—Priceless!

52. Who children are is far more important than what they do. Children are human beings not human doings.

Agape (Love)

(1 Corinthians 13; John 13:35)

53. Unconditional love says, "There is nothing you can do that will make me stop loving you."

54. Right reactions arise from acting like God not acting like our _____.

55. No substitute exists for quality, one-on-one time with children.

56. Your relationship with your child is more important than your being _____.

57. Replace criticism with affirmation.

58. Building on a child's strengths helps him/her overcome _____.

59. _____ a child creates a fearful, angry adult.

60. _____ a child creates a weak, imma-
    ture adult.

61. _____ a child creates a distrusting,
    controlling adult.

62. Forgiveness heals a child's _____.

63. Speak to a child's heart not to their _____.
    Know your child's love languages:

    1. _____

    2. _____

    3. _____

    4. _____

    5. _____

64. Parenting for life is a given; friends for life is hard
    work.

    • When your children become old enough or even
      now select their friends, will you have given them
      any reason to select you?

    • Do your children consider you to be a part of
      their most loyal and desirable relationships?

65. The door of tough love must open both ways.

66. _____ your child before he or she
    repents.

Blessing

67. Don't waste your tears; save them for a river of

_____.

68. A name of blessing is spoken daily over a child;

a _____ child lives with a daily curse.

> *A good name is more desirable than great riches;*
> *to be esteemed is better than silver or gold.* (Proverbs 22:1)

We give our children the name/character/impression that is stamped on our lives. (Revelation 3:12)

1. _____.

2. _____.

3. _____.

How were you named? After the Lord's leading or the world's circumstances. Your name is to be a blessing not a curse.

> *"I will make you into a great nation and I will bless you; I will make your name great, and you will be a blessing. I will bless those who bless you, and whoever curses you I will curse; and all peoples on earth will be blessed through you." Mary & Joseph named Jesus what God called Him; Mary pronounced blessing in the womb; Hannah dedicated Samuel to the Lord.* (Genesis 12:2-3)

69. _____ the Decalogue creates generational curses; obeying the Decalogue creates endless blessings.

Shut Open Doors—Generational Curses

1. No other gods—_____

2. No graven images— _____

3. Don't Profane—_____

4. Keep Sabbath—_____

5. Honor Parents—_____

6. Don't Murder—_____

7. No Adultery—_____

8. Don't Steal—_____

9. Don't Lie—_____

10. Don't Covet—_____

70. The best way to teach prayer is to pray over, often and out loud with children.

71. Teach a child to manage money not _____.

72. Leave a spiritual and material inheritance great enough to bless your seed's seed.

73. Live to please God and bless ('esher) your children instead of blessing ('esher) God and pleasing your children.

74. Children need to learn that God not you is their _____.

75. The fruit of the Spirit in a child grow from the seeds a parent sows.

76. Sow into your children to give them seed not a
   _____.

77. The future of children is not determined by their
   _____; their destiny is determined by God's plan.

7 Action Steps to Healthy Families

1. _____.

2. _____.

3. _____.

4. _____.

5. _____.

6. _____.

7. _____.

Dr. Larry Keefauver, YMCS, PO Box 950596, Lake Mary, FL 32795.
407-330-0410; 407-324-5006 (fax); lkeefauv@bellsouth.net or www.ymcs.org